Acoustic Monitoring Report, Denali National Park and Preserve - 2009

Natural Resource Data Series NPS/DENA/NRDS—2012/271

Jared Withers
Physical Scientist
PO Box 9
Denali National Park, AK 99755

March 2012

U.S. Department of the Interior
National Park Service
Natural Resource Stewardship and Science
Fort Collins, Colorado

The National Park Service, Natural Resource Stewardship and Science office in Fort Collins, Colorado publishes a range of reports that address natural resource topics of interest and applicability to a broad audience in the National Park Service and others in natural resource management, including scientists, conservation and environmental constituencies, and the public.

The Natural Resource Data Series is intended for the timely release of basic data sets and data summaries. Care has been taken to assure accuracy of raw data values, but a thorough analysis and interpretation of the data has not been completed. Consequently, the initial analyses of data in this report are provisional and subject to change.

All manuscripts in the series receive the appropriate level of peer review to ensure that the information is scientifically credible, technically accurate, appropriately written for the intended audience, and designed and published in a professional manner.

This report received informal peer review by subject-matter experts who were not directly involved in the collection, analysis, or reporting of the data. Data in this report were collected and analyzed using methods based on established protocols and were analyzed and interpreted within the guidelines of the protocols.

Views, statements, findings, conclusions, recommendations, and data in this report do not necessarily reflect views and policies of the National Park Service, U.S. Department of the Interior. Mention of trade names or commercial products does not constitute endorsement or recommendation for use by the U.S. Government.

This report is available from the Denali website (http://www.nps.gov/dena/naturescience/index.htm), the Central Alaska Network website (http://science.nature.nps.gov/im/units/cakn/) and the Natural Resource Publications Management website (http://www.nature.nps.gov/publications/nrpm).

Please cite this publication as:

Withers, J. 2012. Acoustic monitoring report, Denali National Park and Preserve - 2009. Natural Resource Data Series NPS/DENA/NRDS—2012/271. National Park Service, Fort Collins, Colorado.

NPS 184/113341, March 2012

Contents

Contents (continued)

Figures

Figures (continued)

Figures (continued)

Figures (continued)

Tables

Executive Summary

Park staff deployed acoustic monitoring systems to ten locations in Denali National Park and Preserve in 2009. The purpose of this monitoring effort was to inventory the acoustic conditions and level of aircraft operations in Denali National Park as called for in the 2006 Backcountry Management Plan. Data collected included existing ambient sound pressure levels, natural ambient sound pressure levels, percent time audible, and loud acoustic event statistics for intrinsic and extrinsic sound sources. Deployed systems were configured to log sound pressure levels every second and continuous mp3 audio recordings, 24 hours per day. These data serve as a permanent record of existing acoustical conditions at these locations for the summer of 2009.

Table 1 shows summarized results of 2009 monitoring, including existing and natural ambient sound statistics in dBA (A-weighted decibels) and average percentage of time audible, number of events per day, and maximum sound pressure level (SPL) for aircraft sound sources, which are the most prominent extrinsic sound at these sites. Median existing ambient (L_{50}) describes the acoustical environment as is, including both natural and extrinsic sounds. Natural ambient (L_{nat}) estimates what the acoustical environment might sound like without the contribution of extrinsic sounds. This table also shows exceedence metrics L_{10} and L_{90}, which essentially mark the average maximum and minimum exceedence levels over the monitoring periods.

Table 1. Median natural sound, existing ambient sound, and mean aircraft statistics for all sites*.

Site Name	L_{nat}	L_{10}	L_{50}	L_{90}	% Aircraft	# Aircraft/Day	Aircraft Max SPL
Castle Rocks	19.35	23.45	19.35	18.35	0.83	2.6	37.9
Center Alaska	20.05	27.00	24.70	22.25	1.20	9.2	40.9
Dunkle Hills[1]	-	-	-	-	1.9	-	-
Herron River	24.65	28.40	24.70	22.25	1.20	3.3	34.9
Lower Slippery Creek	18.35	20.35	18.40	17.60	2.54	6.8	34.5
Triple Lakes	26.95	32.25	27.45	24.55	11.75	53.0	45.1
Upper Tokositna Glacier	36.75	39.25	36.85	35.35	5.97	28.5	51.7
Upper Traleika Glacier	30.95	32.30	31.10	29.65	4.85	27.0	50.1
Upper West Branch Toklat	32.70	36.15	32.80	31.60	3.66	20.5	52.3

*L_{nat}, L_{10}, L_{50}, L_{90}, and SPL in dBA.   [1] : Winter season site. SPL data was unusable.

When interpreting sound pressure level data, it should be noted that the decibel scale is logarithmic. As such, a three decibel increase in sound pressure level is actually a doubling of sound energy. Overall, the acoustic conditions of these 2009 sites varied. The Lower Slippery Creek site experienced the lowest ambient and natural ambient sound levels. Very low levels of aircraft activity were observed at Castle Rocks.

Introduction

Natural sound is both a resource in its own right as well as an important aspect of Denali National Park and Preserve's (Denali) wilderness resource values, and the influence of motorized noise on visitor experience is a key concern throughout the park. Denali's Backcountry Management Plan (BCMP), finalized in 2006, established indicators and standards for the natural sound environment and called for monitoring to evaluate whether the standards are being satisfied. Soundscape measurements are objective and employ methods for monitoring that are easily reviewed by the public, which will provide strong support for future management decisions. Without these data, the park will have little information to make management guidelines or support management decisions that may affect the quality of Denali's soundscape.

The initial push for Denali to begin soundscape inventories began with Director's Order 47 (DO-47). Robert Stanton issued the order in 2000 directing park managers to identify baseline soundscapes and related measures. DO-47 states that "natural sounds are intrinsic elements of the environment that are often associated with parks and park purposes...They are inherent components of 'the scenery and the natural and historic objects and the wild life' protected by the NPS Organic Act." DO-47 directed park managers to "(1) measure baseline acoustic conditions, (2) determine which existing or proposed human-made sounds are consistent with park purposes, (3) set acoustic management goals and objectives based on those purposes, and (4) determine which noise sources are impacting the park and need to be addressed by management." Furthermore, it requires park managers to "(1) evaluate and address self-generated noise, and (2) constructively engage with those responsible for other noise sources that impact parks to explore what can be done to better protect parks." (NPS 2000).

The primary purpose behind the Denali soundscape study has been to measure the level of influence overflight traffic and snowmachine traffic has on the Park's soundscape. Understanding the natural soundscape is important to evaluate the level of impact human-generated sounds may have on this important resource. The natural soundscape is generally comprised of two main sound categories, physical and biological. Physical sounds are created by physical forces (wind, rock fall, rivers, etc.), whereas biological sounds are created by organisms (birds, frogs, plants, etc.). The presence and abundance of sounds from these two categories is used to characterize different habitats. (Dunholter et al. 1989) Different habitats have specific soundscape characteristics that are an important attribute of the natural system, with distinct impacts on the human perception of the environment. Impacts on the natural soundscape and on visitor experiences come from human-generated sounds.

Soundscape Planning Authorities

The National Park Service (NPS) Organic Act of 1916 states that the purpose of national parks is "... to conserve the scenery and the natural and historic objects and the wild life therein and to provide for the enjoyment of the same in such manner and by such means as will leave them unimpaired for the enjoyment of future generations." (NPS 1916) In addition to the NPS Organic Act, the Redwoods Act of 1978 affirmed that, "the protection, management, and administration of these areas shall be conducted in light of the high value and integrity of the National Park System and shall not be exercised in derogation of the values and purposes for which these various areas have been established, except as may have been or shall be directly and specifically provided by Congress." (NPS 1978)

Direction for management of natural soundscapes[1] is represented in 2006 Management Policy 4.9:

> "The Service will restore to the natural condition wherever possible those park soundscapes that have become degraded by unnatural sounds (noise), and will protect natural soundscapes from unacceptable impacts. Using appropriate management planning, superintendents will identify what levels and types of unnatural sound constitute acceptable impacts on park natural soundscapes. The frequencies, magnitudes, and durations of acceptable levels of unnatural sound will vary throughout a park, being generally greater in developed areas. In and adjacent to parks, the Service will monitor human activities that generate noise that adversely affects park soundscapes [acoustic resources], including noise caused by mechanical or electronic devices. The Service will take action to prevent or minimize all noise that through frequency, magnitude, or duration adversely affects the natural soundscape [acoustic resource] or other park resources or values, or that exceeds levels that have been identified through monitoring as being acceptable to or appropriate for visitor uses at the sites being monitored" (NPS 2006a).

It should be noted that the Management Policy 8.2.3: Use of Motorized Equipment states "the natural ambient sound level—that is, the environment of sound that exists in the absence of human-caused noise—is the baseline condition, and the standard against which current conditions in a soundscape [acoustic resource] will be measured and evaluated" (NPS 2006b). However, the desired acoustic condition may also depend upon the resources and the values of the park. For instance, "culturally appropriate sounds are important elements of the national park experience in many parks" (NPS 2006b). In this case, "the Service will preserve soundscape resources and values of the parks to the greatest extent possible to protect opportunities for appropriate transmission of cultural and historic sounds that are fundamental components of the purposes and values for which the parks were established" (NPS 2006b).

Sampling Plan
Denali's soundscape sampling plan was designed using a coarse grid derived from the Long Term Ecological Monitoring (LTEM) grid (NPS 2006c). The number of points sampled in the coarse grid is driven by the number of acoustic monitoring stations available (five), and the length of time each station should be established at each location. To properly characterize the natural soundscape, stations should be established such that at least one month of continuous data is collected at each site during the field/tourist season (Ambrose and Burson 2004). To maximize the spatial coverage with only five stations it was decided to sample two locations through the entire field season, while rotating three stations over two sites each – two months as each site. Four of the two month-long sites would be established on the LTEM sampling grid, with two free to allow park managers to collect data at sites of specific interest which may not fall on a grid point. As such, six LTEM grid locations will be sampled each year, with 60 grid points to be sampled overall (Figure 1). In addition, opportunistic sampling may be attempted

---

[1] The 2006 Management Policy 4.9 and related documents refer to "soundscapes" instead of "acoustic resources." When quoting from this authority, it is advisable to note that the term often refers to resources rather than visitor perceptions.

during the winter months as permitted by funding, personnel, and ease of access to provide some indication of acoustic conditions outside the field/tourist season.

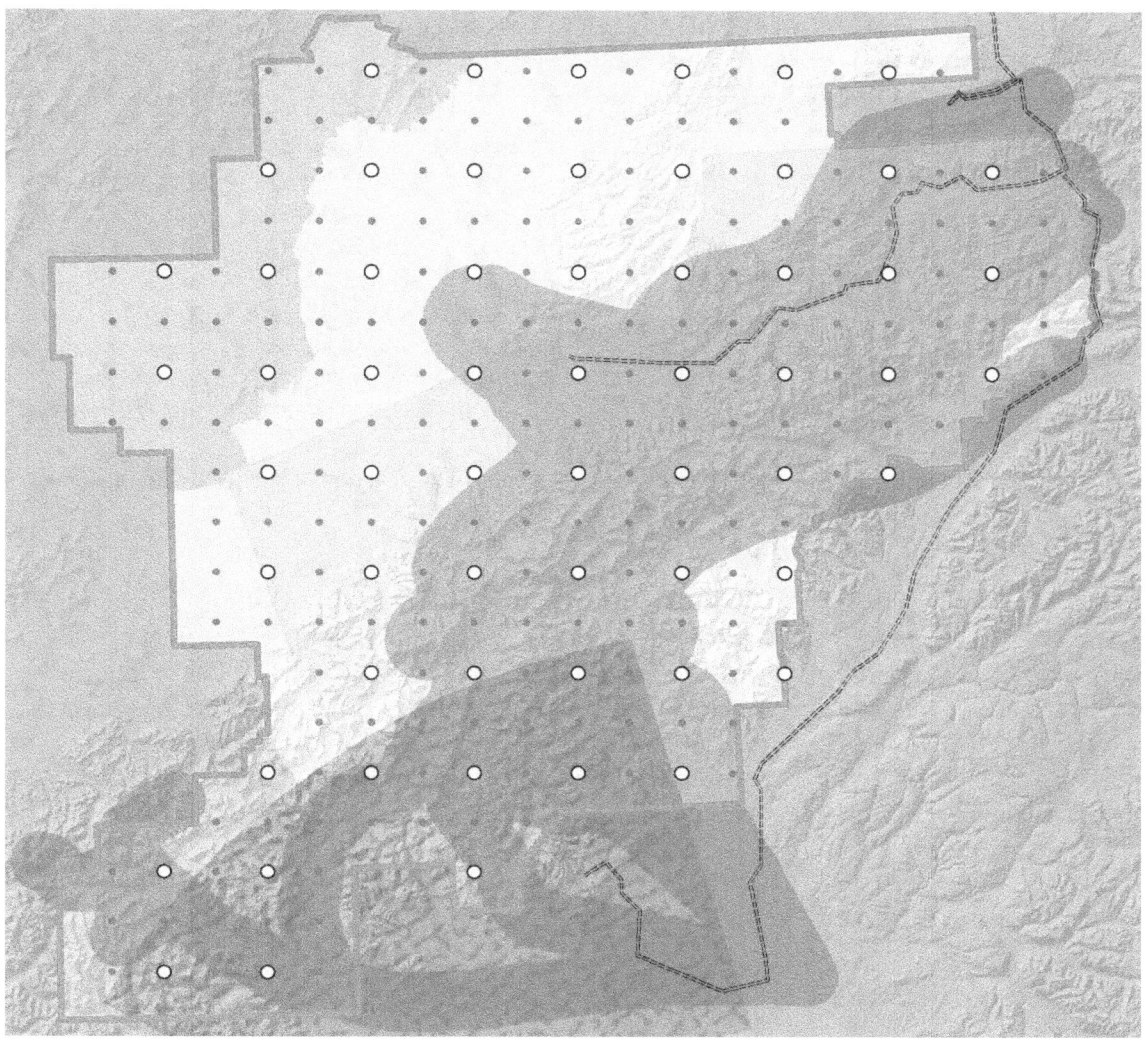

Figure 1. Map showing the coarse grid of sixty points to be sampled, marked by yellow dots.

Study Area

Park staff deployed acoustic monitoring systems to nine locations in Denali National Park in 2009, as shown in Table 3 and Figure 2.

Table 2. Sites sampled in 2009.

Site Location	Elevation (meters)	Latitude	Longitude	Sampling Period*
Castle Rocks	325	63.45519	-152.04146	Jun-28 to July-29
Center Alaska	207	63.80506	-152.01262	May-29 to Jun-27
Dunkle Hills[1]	828	63.26699	-149.54153	Mar-27 to Apr-04
Herron River	490	63.26059	-152.05447	Jul-30 to Spet-01
Lower Slippery Creek	365	63.62359	-151.24017	Jul-20 to Sept-16
Triple Lakes	654	63.66258	-148.87473	Jun-30 to Aug-06
Upper Tokositna Glacier	1025	62.88184	-150.88486	Aug-17 to Sept-15
Upper Traleika Glacier	2537	63.07688	-150.82539	Jun-10 to Jul-13
Upper West Branch Toklat	1224	63.40927	-150.03561	Aug-11 to Sept-07

[1] : Winter season site.

*One month of continuous data is the goal, but some sites do not achieve this goal do to equipment failure, animal tampering, insufficient solar radiation, and access scheduling. If a full month of data was not collected, an acoustic profile is compiled using the available data.

A tenth site was attempted at 14,000' base camp on Mt. McKinley's West Buttress climbing route. The equipment for this installation was packaged to be light weight and compact, powered by disposable alkaline batteries. An error was made when calculating the number of batteries required to power the station, and as a consequence it only collected data for two days. These two days of data do not cover the range of variability in acoustic conditions likely experienced at this location, which are influenced by wind, cloud cover, flight schedules, etc. The decision was made to drop this small dataset, and resample the site in 2010.

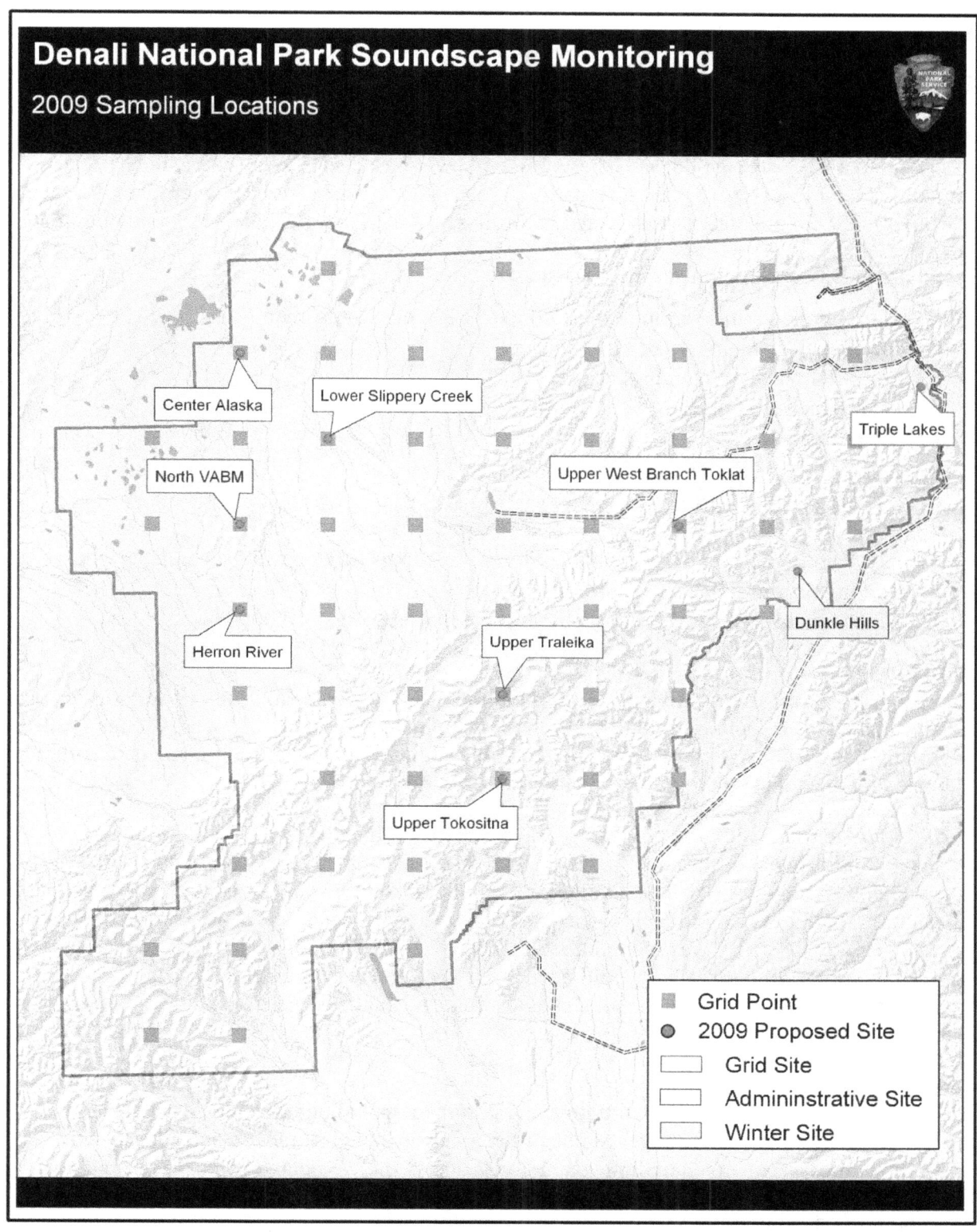

Figure 2. 2009 Acoustic monitoring sites in Denali National Park.

Methods

Automated Monitoring

The Larson Davis 831 sound level meter (SLM) is a hardware-based, real-time analyzer which constantly records one second sound pressure level (SPL) and 1/3 octave band data, and exports these data to a USB storage device. These Larson Davis-based sites met American National Standards Institute (ANSI) Type 1 standards (ANSI 1992, 1968). To supplement the SPL data, Edirol R-09HR field recorders make mp3 recordings via the Larson Davis 831 audio output.

Each Larson Davis sampling station consisted of:

- Microphone with environmental shroud and Rycote windscreen
- Preamplifier
- Edirol R-09HR mp3 recorder
- Solar panel and batteries
- Anemometer

Each acoustic sampling station collected:

- SPL data in the form of A-weighted decibel readings (dBA) every second
- Continuous digital audio recordings
- 1/3 octave band data every second ranging from 12.5 Hz – 20,000 Hz

Visual Analysis

For each monitoring site, staff visually analyzed thirty days of collected SPL samples in order to identify the frequency and durations of mechanized sound sources. See Appendix C for further information on visual analysis. Hourly time audible statistics are then used to calculate natural ambient sound level estimates (see Calculation of Metrics below).

Audibility Analysis

For each monitoring site, staff analyzed a subset of audio samples (every other day of the thirty days which were analyzed visually) to identify natural and quiet sound sources which are difficult to reliably identify though visual analysis. Listening headphones are calibrated with a 94dB, 1000Hz tone which was recorded at the time of data collection. This approximates a playback volume similar to what would be heard if the observer were actually listening at the sample site. This audibility data results in an estimate of total percent time audible and makeup of the natural components of the soundscape.

Calculation of Metrics

Several metrics are calculated in order to provide some detail about the characteristics of the acoustical environment. The current status of the acoustical environment can be characterized by a number of measurements including sound levels across the 1/3 octave band spectrum (from 12.5 Hz to 20,000 Hz), overall sound levels, and percent time audible durations for various sound sources. Two fundamental descriptors of the acoustic environment are existing ambient and natural ambient sound levels which are presented as exceedence levels (L_x). They represent the dBA exceeded x percent of the time during the given measurement period. For example, measured in dBA, the existing ambient (L_{50}) is the sound level exceeded 50% of the time, or median sound level. It is the uncensored composite of all sounds at a site, both human caused and natural. The natural ambient (L_{nat}) estimates the acoustic environment without the contribution of anthropogenic sounds. L_{10} and L90 are also presented which describe the sound levels exceeded 10% and 90% of the time, respectively.

The differences between L_{50} and L_{nat} values allow NPS to answer the following questions:
1. What are the listening opportunities in the absence of human development and activities?
2. How are these listening opportunities compromised by increased sound levels due to noise?

To calculate L_{nat}, the following method is utilized:

- NPS staff calculate the percentage of all samples containing extrinsic sounds for each hour of the day (P_H) by either listening to samples, or visually analyzing daily spectrograms.
- P_H is used to complete this formula for every hour: $x = \dfrac{1 - P_H}{2} + P_H$
- Hourly x_H values are entered into a database of all octave band information.
- Example: if extrinsic sounds are audible 50% of the time ($P_H = 0.5$), then x_H is 0.75.
- L_{nat} is computed as the sound level that is exceeded $100 * x_H$ percent of the time.
(In practice, L_{nat} is calculated by sorting the relevant sound level measurements and using x_H to extract the appropriate order statistic).

This procedure approximates the sound levels that would have been measured in the absence of extrinsic noise. The procedure is guaranteed to produce an estimate that is equal to or below the existing ambient sound levels, and the results of this calculation have produced consistent results at most backcountry sites analyzed by the NPS Natural Sounds Program. (NPS 2008)

Results

Table 3 is a summary of 2009 data. Presented are the existing and natural ambient sound statistics in dBA and average percentage of time audible, number of events per day, and maximum sound pressure level (SPL) for aircraft sound sources, which are the most prominent extrinsic sound at these sites. Median existing ambient (L_{50}) describes the acoustical environment as is, including both natural and extrinsic sounds. Natural ambient (L_{nat}) estimates what the acoustical environment might sound like without the contribution of extrinsic sounds. This table also shows exceedence metrics L_{10} and L_{90}, which essentially mark the average maximum and minimum exceedence levels over the monitoring periods.

Table 3. Median natural and existing ambient sound* and mean aircraft statistics for all sites.

Site Name	L_{nat}	L_{10}	L_{50}	L_{90}	% Aircraft	# Aircraft/Day	Aircraft Max SPL
Castle Rocks	19.35	23.45	19.35	18.35	0.83	2.6	37.9
Center Alaska	20.05	27.00	24.70	22.25	1.20	9.2	40.9
Dunkle Hills[1]	-	-	-	-	1.9	-	-
Herron River	24.65	28.40	24.70	22.25	1.20	3.3	34.9
Lower Slippery Creek	18.35	20.35	18.40	17.60	2.54	6.8	34.5
Triple Lakes	26.95	32.25	27.45	24.55	11.75	53.0	45.1
Upper Tokositna Glacier	36.75	39.25	36.85	35.35	5.97	28.5	51.7
Upper Traleika Glacier	30.95	32.30	31.10	29.65	4.85	27.0	50.1
Upper West Branch Toklat	32.70	36.15	32.80	31.60	3.66	20.5	52.3

*L_{nat}, L_{10}, L_{50}, L_{90}, and SPL in dBA.   [1]: Winter season site. SPL data was unusable.

When interpreting sound pressure level data, it should be noted that the decibel scale is logarithmic. As such, a three decibel increase in sound pressure level is actually a doubling of acoustical energy. Overall, the acoustic conditions of these 2009 sites varied. The Lower Slippery Creek site experienced the lowest ambient and natural ambient sound levels. Very low levels of aircraft activity were observed at Castle Rocks.

The following summaries and figures represent the reduced data for each of the 2009 sites. These include percent audibility for natural sounds and mechanized noise, hourly natural ambient and exceedence sound levels, and figures which speak directly to the soundscape indicators and standards outlined in Denali's Backcountry Management Plan: percentage of time audible, number of events per day, and maximum sound pressure levels. (NPS 2006c) A separate section is devoted to each site, and should be considered a comprehensive site profile for Denali purposes.

Location Description: 3.5km North-Northeast of VABM #2079 (Castle).

Purpose/Project: Location randomly chosen from the LTEM grid as part of the long-term Denali Soundscape inventorying and monitoring sampling plan.

Coordinates: Lat. 63.45519, Long. 152.04146   Elevation: 325 meters

BCMP Management Zone: Low   Park Ecoregion: Eolian Lowlands

Time at Location: 28-June-2009 – 29-July-2009

Access: Helicopter

Summary/Notes: The purpose of the North Vertical Angle Benchmark location was to collect data at one of the long-term ecological monitoring (LTEM) grid points, as outlined in the above sampling plan. LTEM grid point #148 was stratified as a New Park location and randomly selected from all locations requiring aircraft access.

The most commonly heard sounds at this site were water (audible 75% of the time), birds (48%), wind (27%), and insects (19%). Human made sound was audible 0.8% of the time on average. Conditions exceeded the BCMP percent audible standard 7% of the time, number of events per day 61% of the time, and maximum SPL 35% of the time.

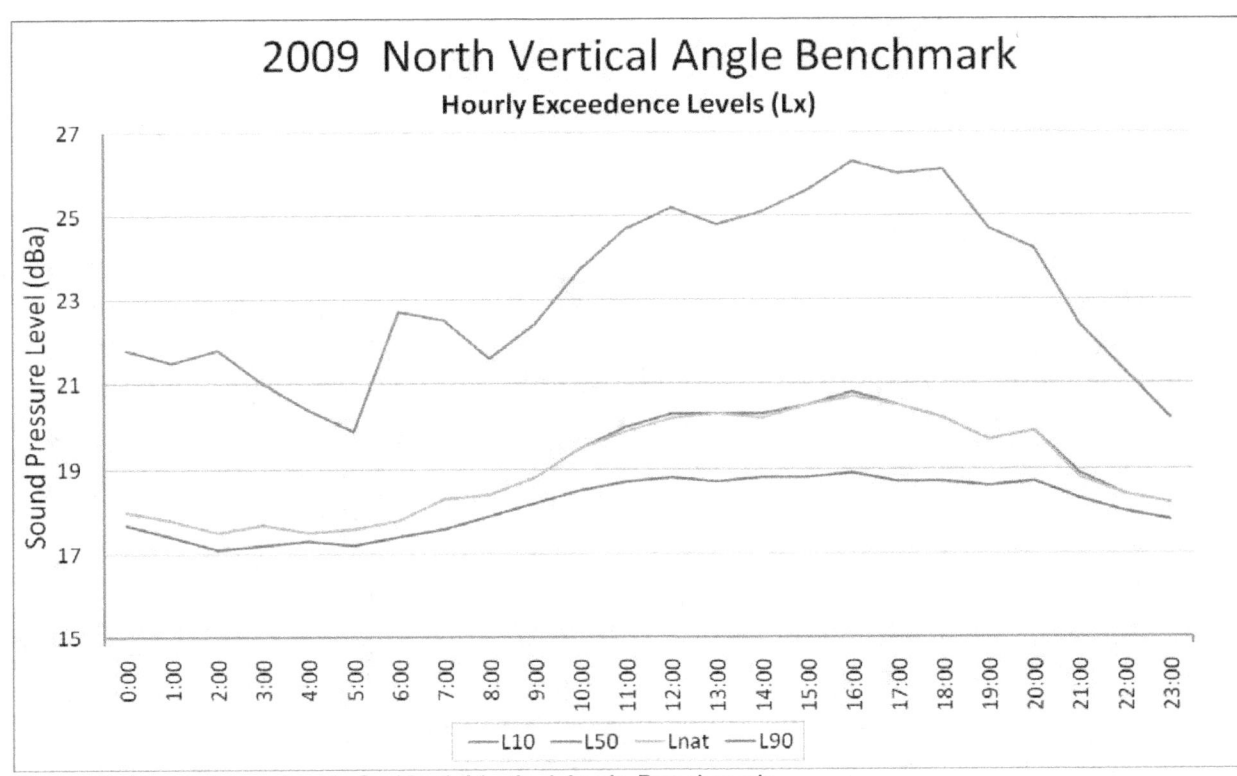

Figure 3. Exceedence levels for North Vertical Angle Benchmark.

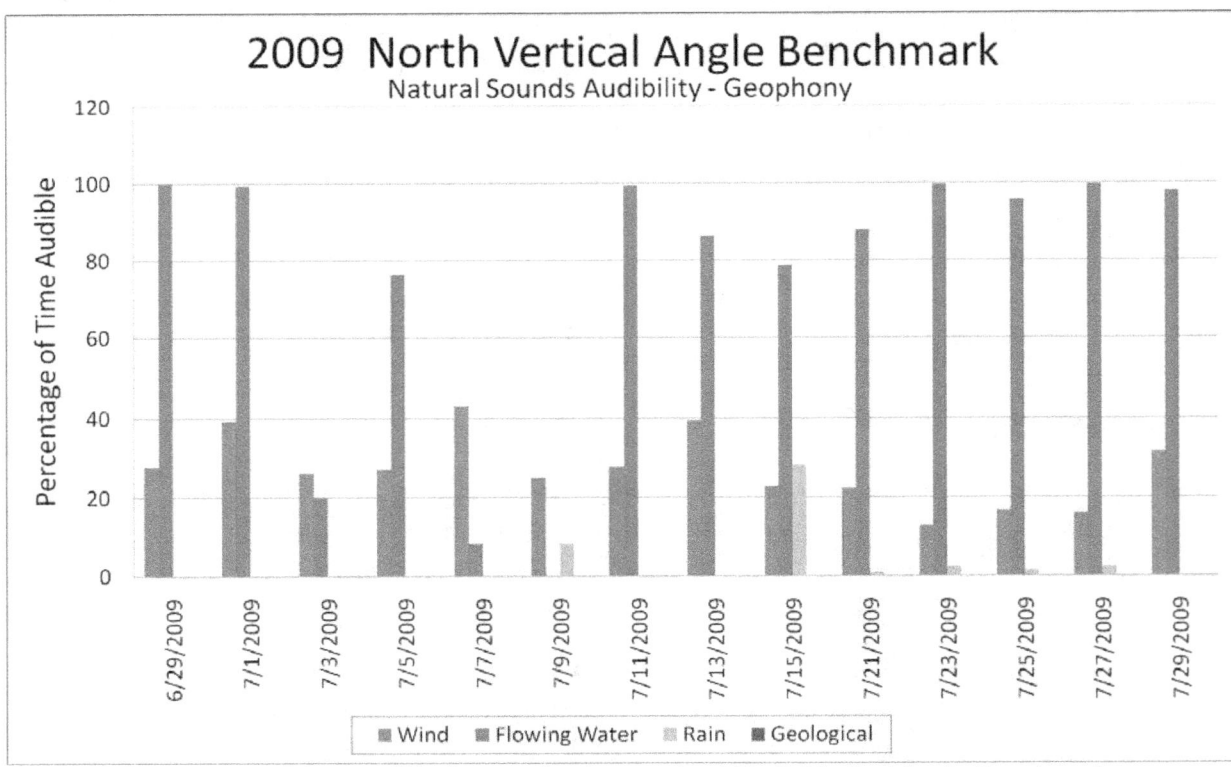

Figure 4. Percentage of time audible for geophonic sounds at North Vertical Angle Benchmark.

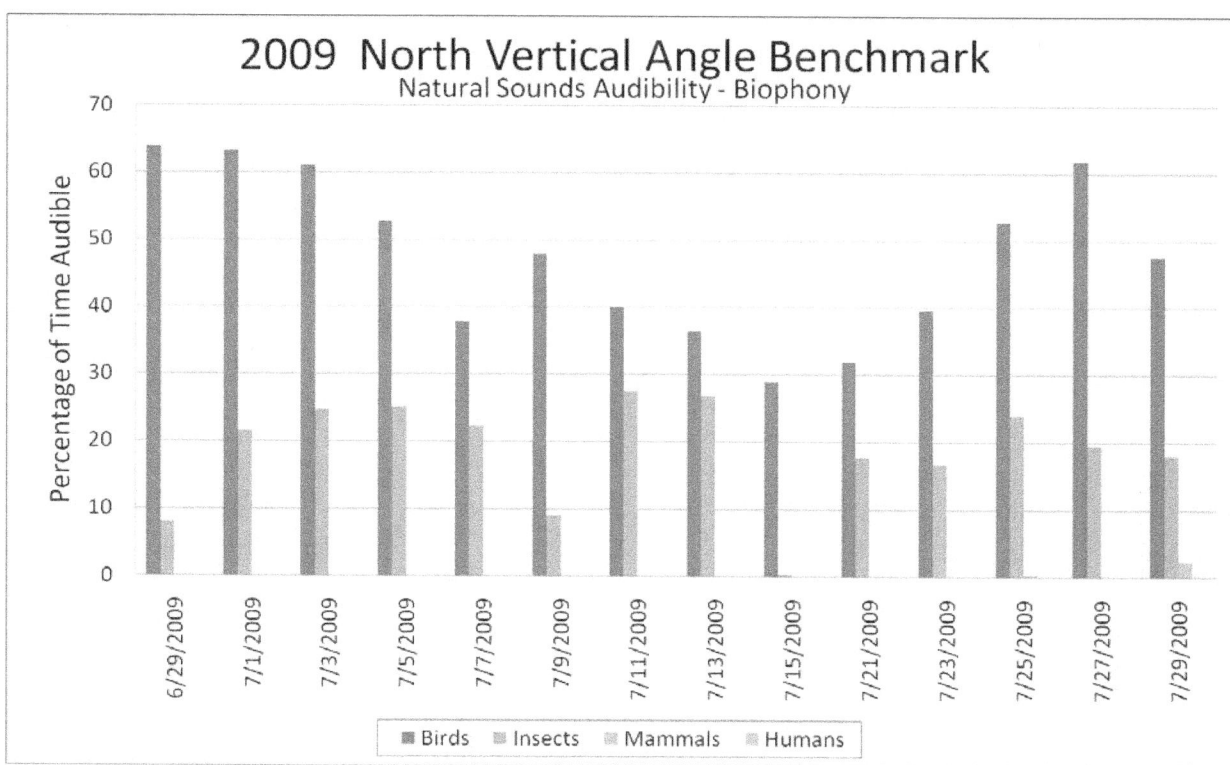

Figure 5. Percentage of time audible for biophonic sounds at North Vertical Angle Benchmark.

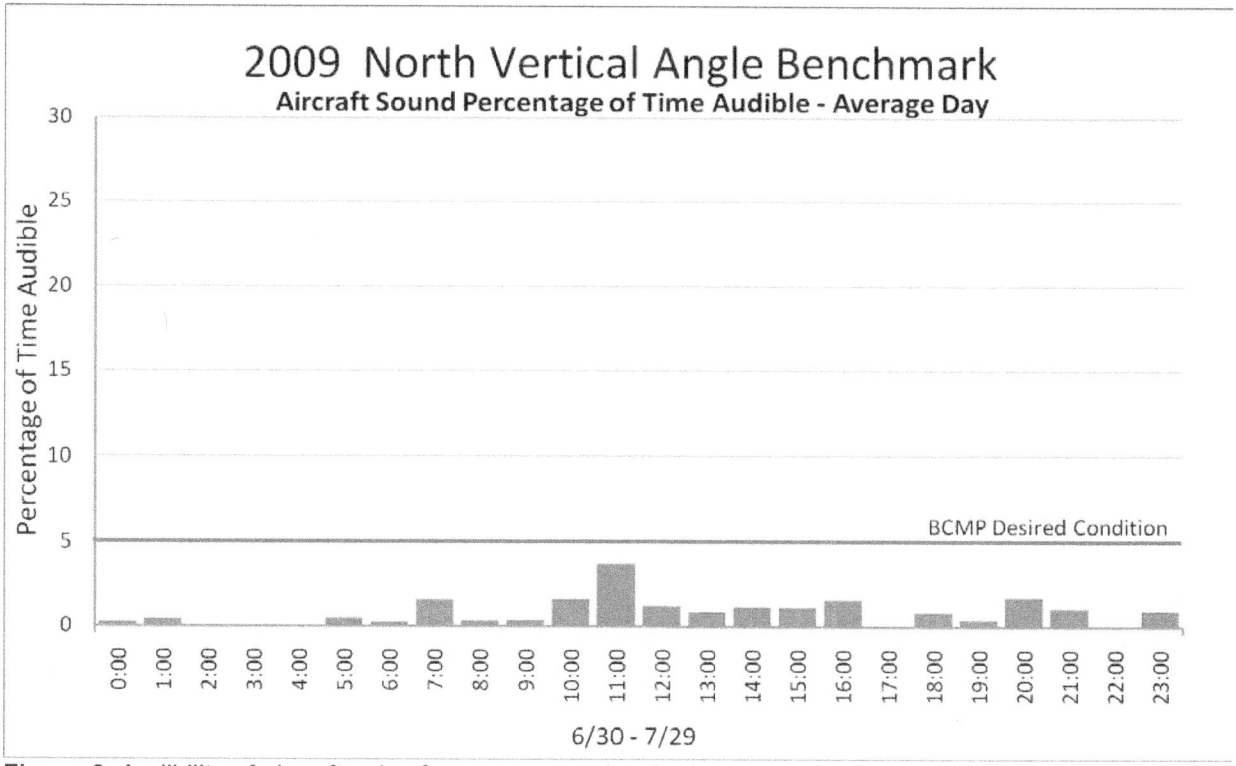

Figure 6. Audibility of aircraft noise for an average day, by hour, at North Vertical Angle Benchmark.

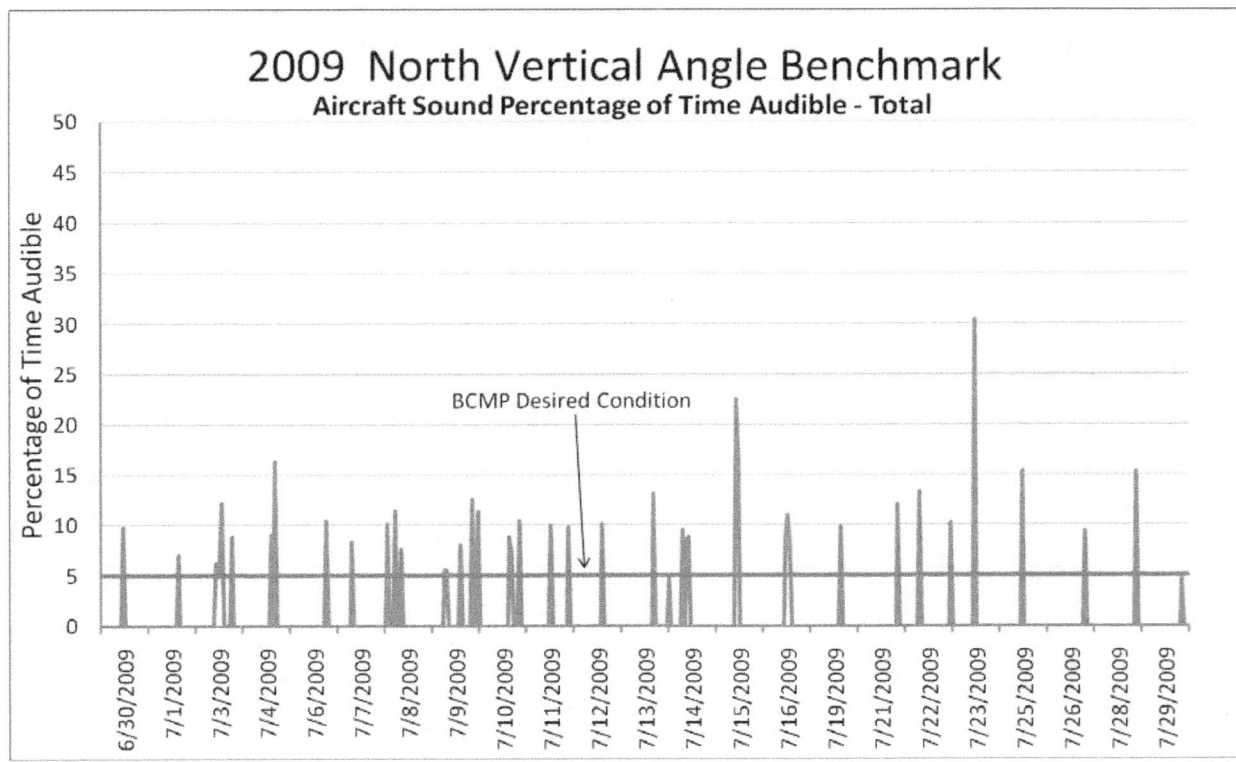

Figure 7. Audibility of aircraft noise at North Vertical Angle Benchmark.

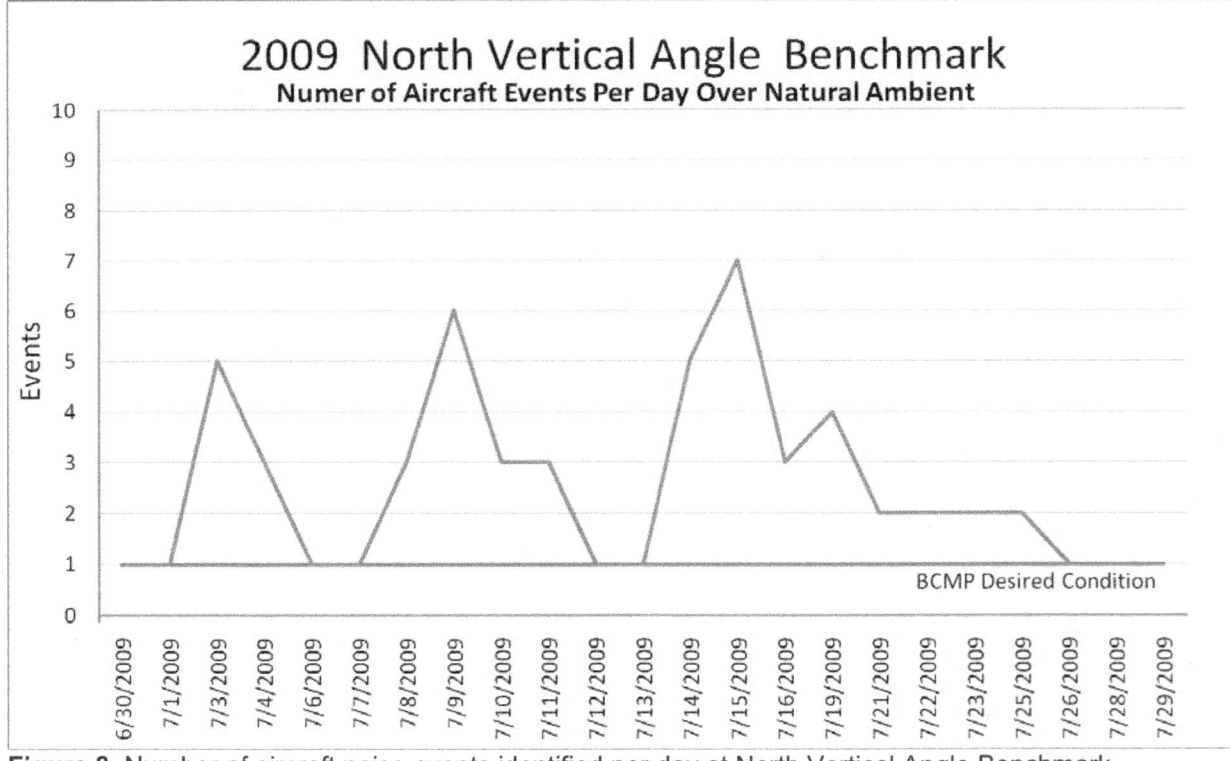

Figure 8. Number of aircraft noise events identified per day at North Vertical Angle Benchmark.

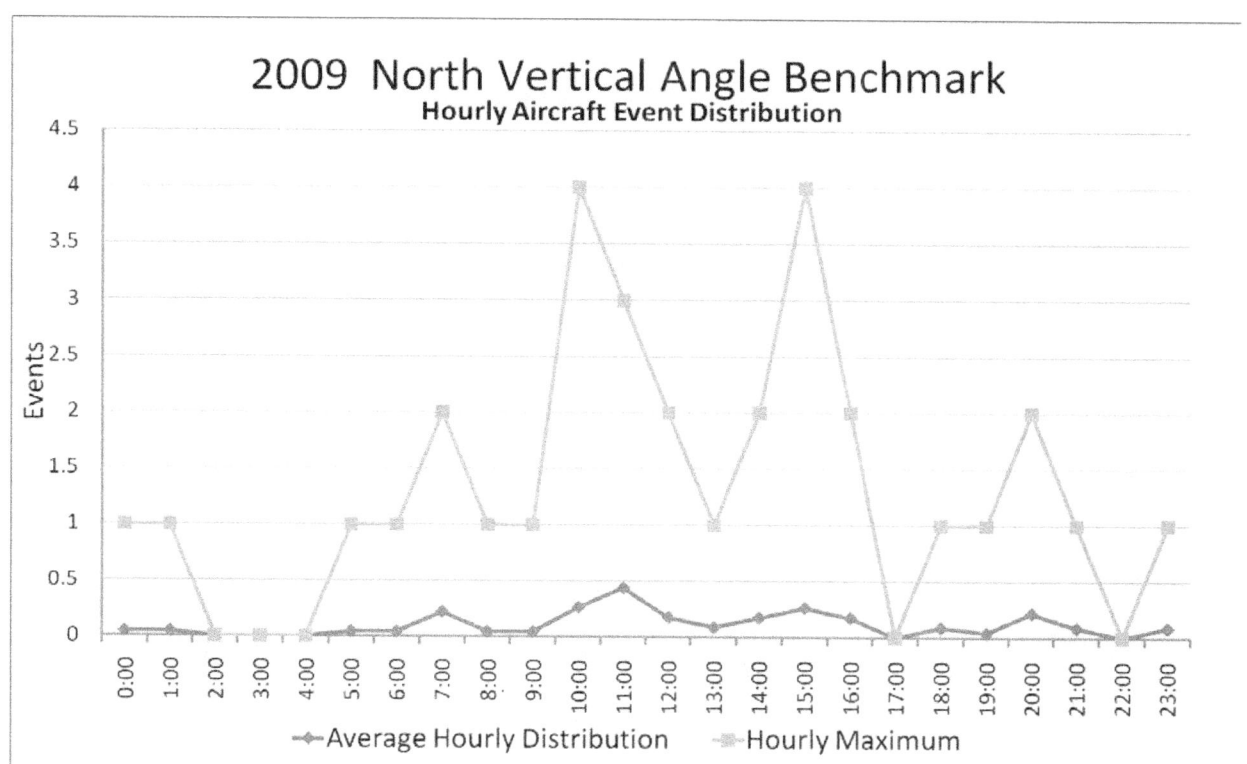

Figure 9. Hourly average and maximum aircraft event distribution at North Vertical Angle Benchmark.

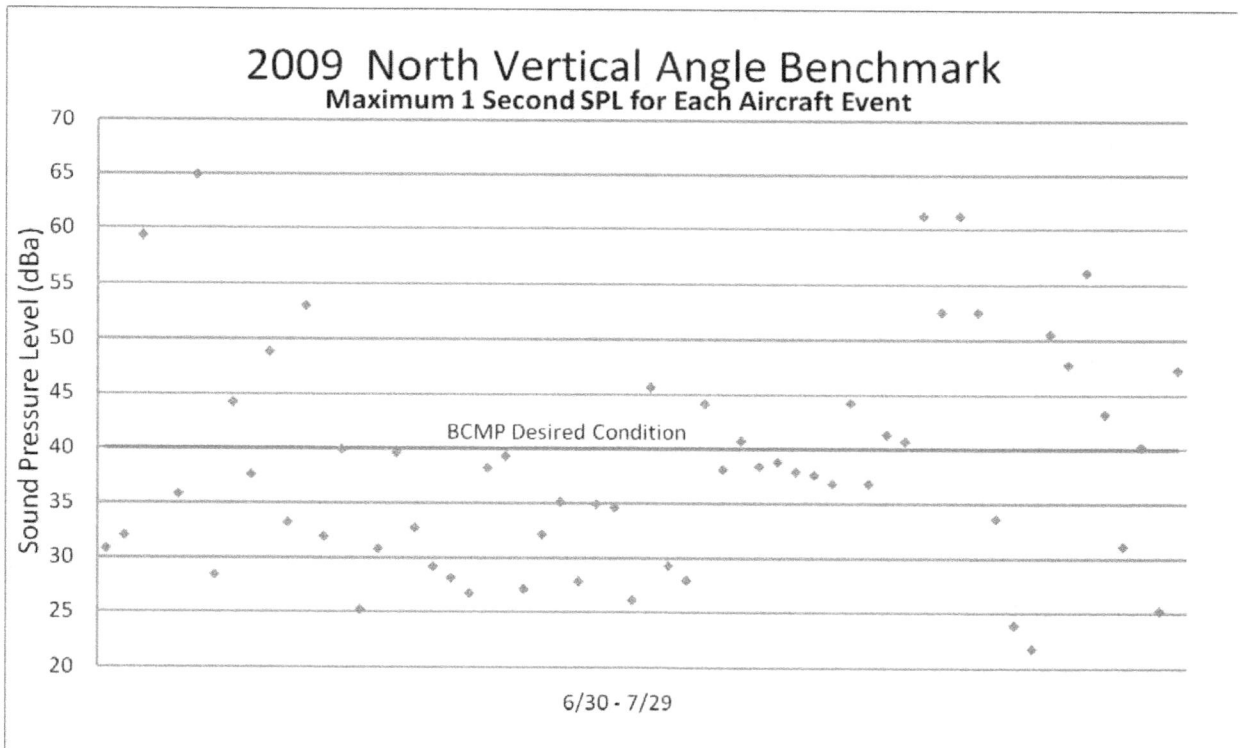

Figure 9. Maximum one-second SPL for each aircraft event identified at North Vertical Angle Benchmark.

Center Alaska

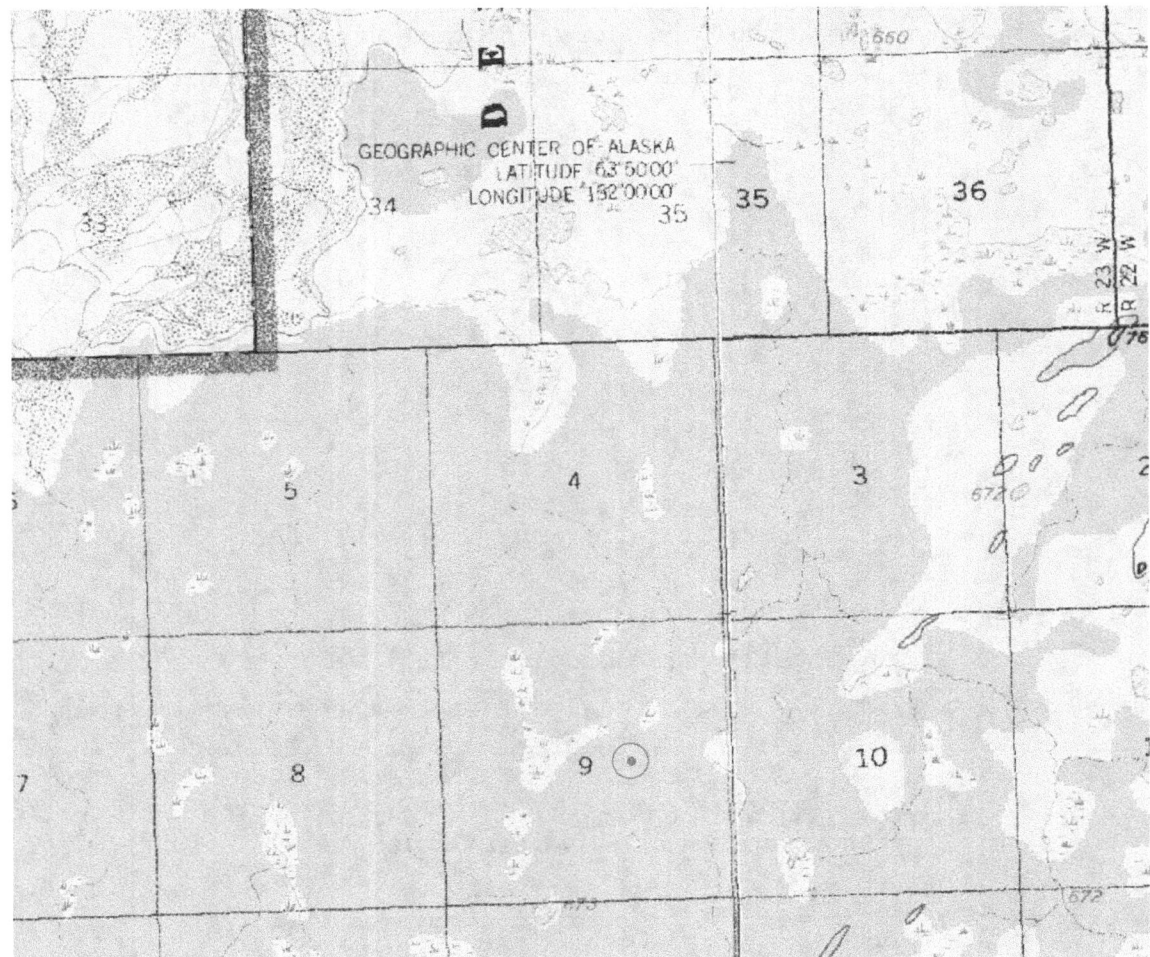

Location Description: ~3.5Km South of the geographic center of Alaska.

Purpose/Project: Location randomly chosen from the LTEM grid as part of the long-term Denali Soundscape inventorying and monitoring sampling plan.

Coordinates: Lat. 63.80506, Long. 152.01262   Elevation: 207 Meters

Time at Location: 29-May-2009 – 27-June-2009

BCMP Management Zone: Low   Park Ecoregion: Minchumina Basin Lowlands

Access: Helicopter

Summary: The purpose of the Center Alaska location was to collect data at one of the long-term ecological monitoring (LTEM) grid points, as outlined in the above sampling plan. LTEM grid point #227 was stratified as a New Park location and randomly selected from all locations requiring aircraft access.

The most commonly heard sounds at this site were birds (audible 80% of the time), wind (43%), insects (15%), and rain (6%). Human made sound was audible 2.4% of the time on average. Conditions exceeded the BCMP percent audible standard 23% of the time, number of events per day 100% of the time, and maximum SPL 55% of the time.

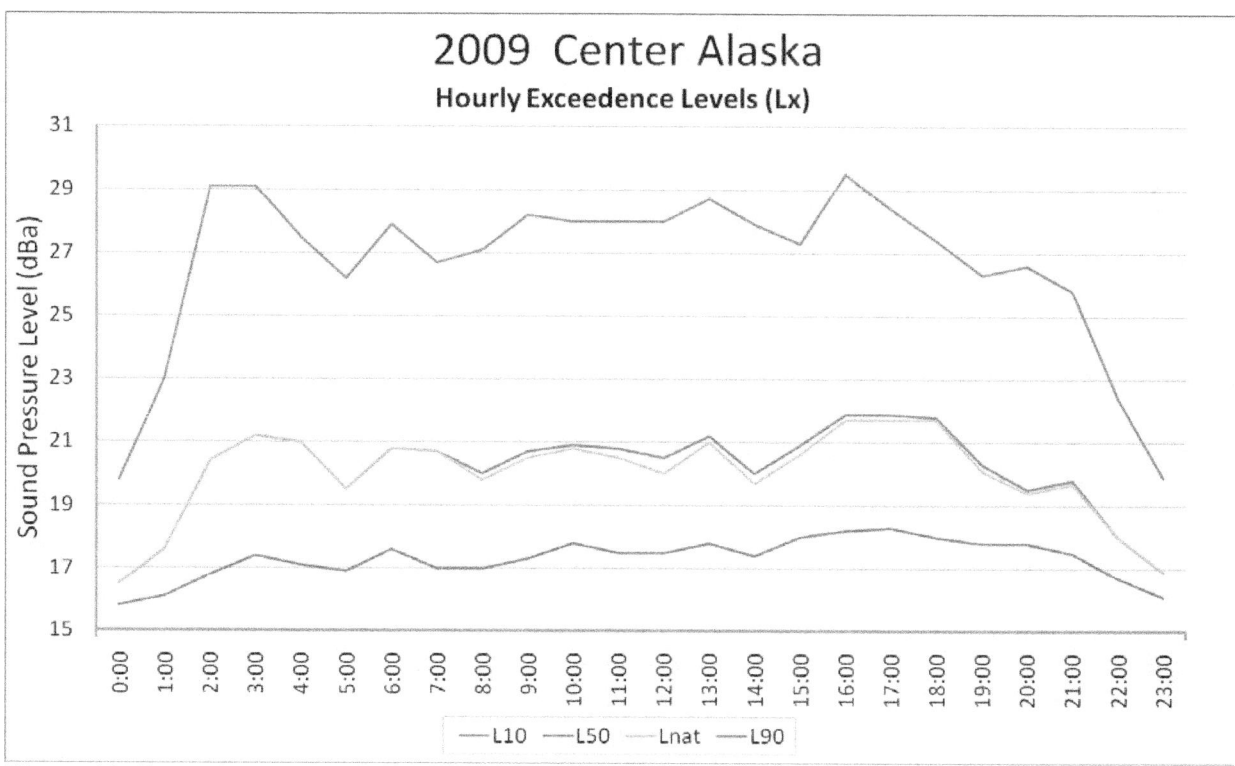

Figure 10. Exceedence levels for Center Alaska.

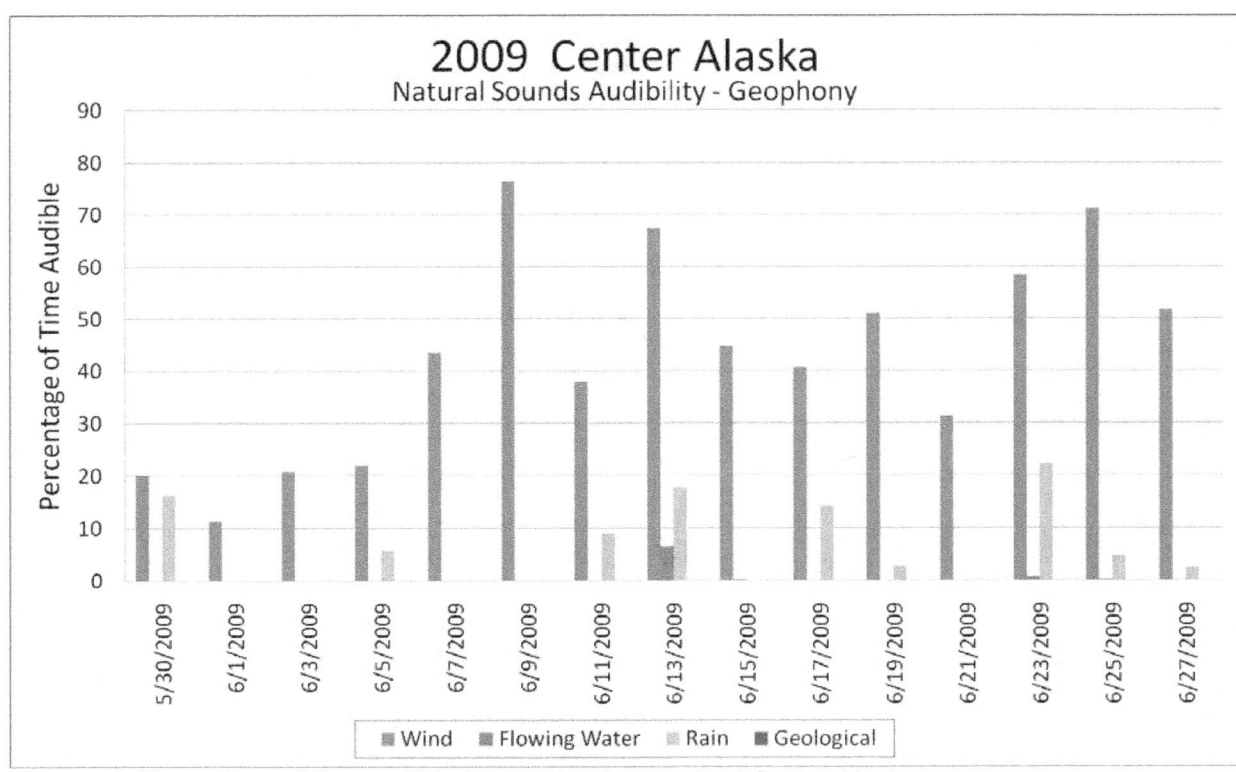

Figure 11. Percentage of time audible for geophonic sounds at Center Alaska.

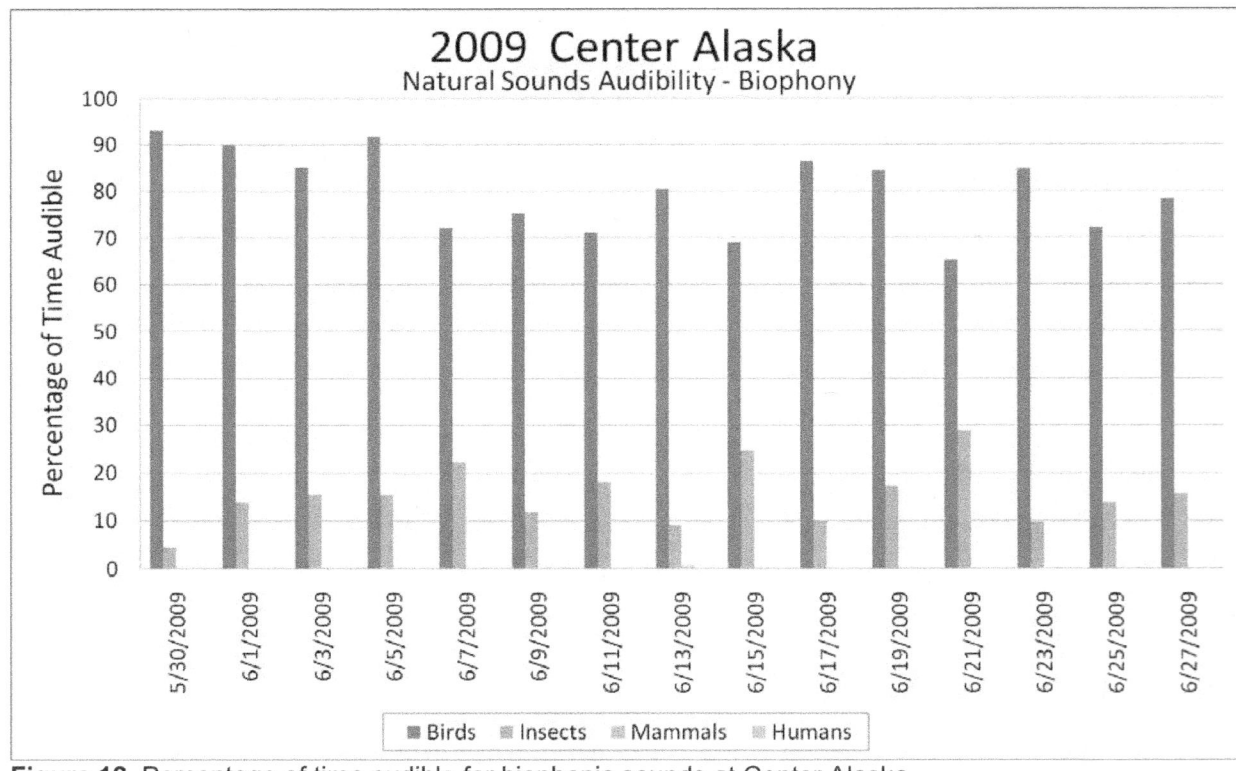

Figure 12. Percentage of time audible for biophonic sounds at Center Alaska.

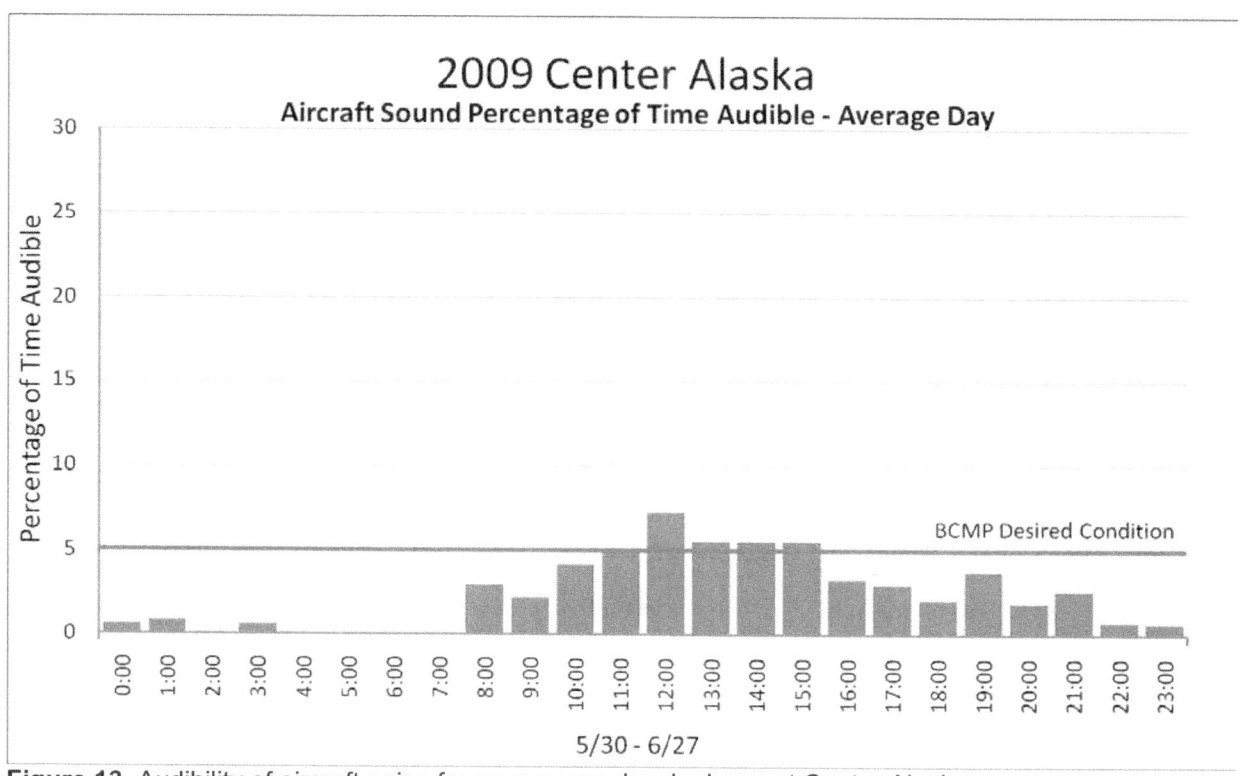

Figure 13. Audibility of aircraft noise for an average day, by hour, at Center Alaska.

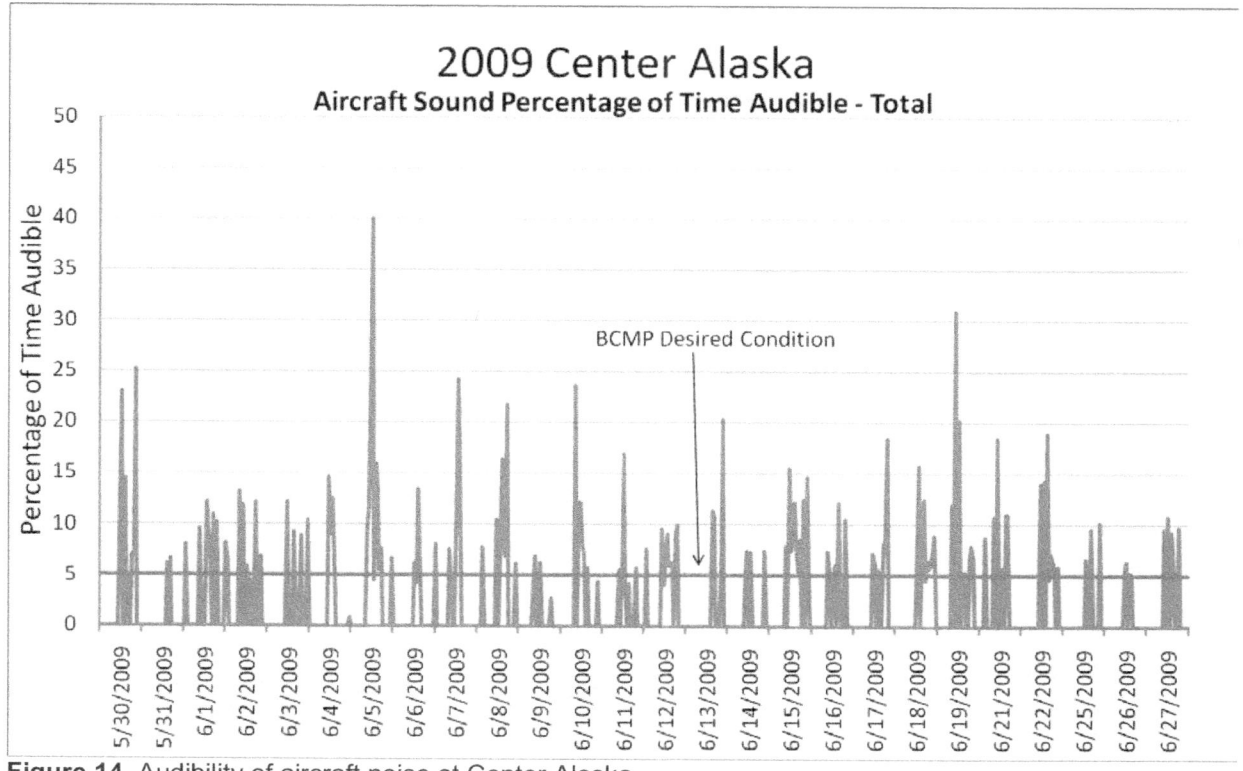

Figure 14. Audibility of aircraft noise at Center Alaska

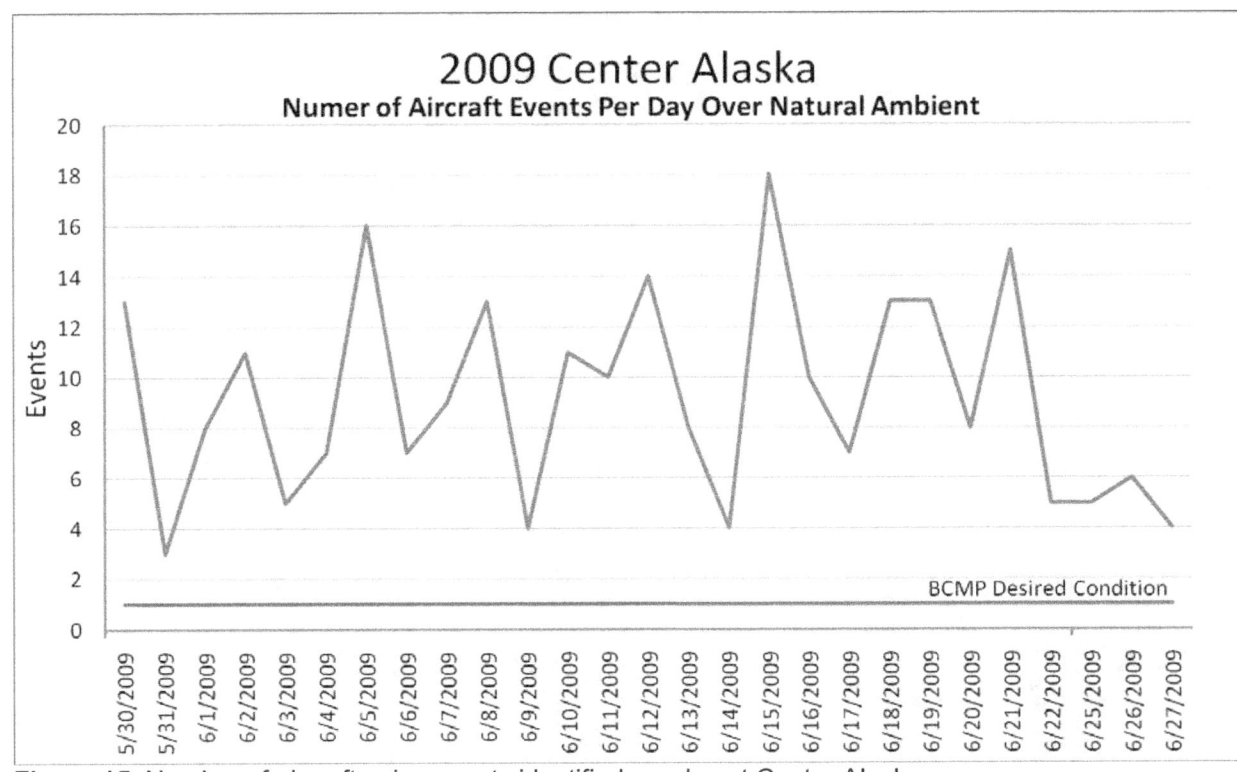

Figure 15. Number of aircraft noise events identified per day at Center Alaska.

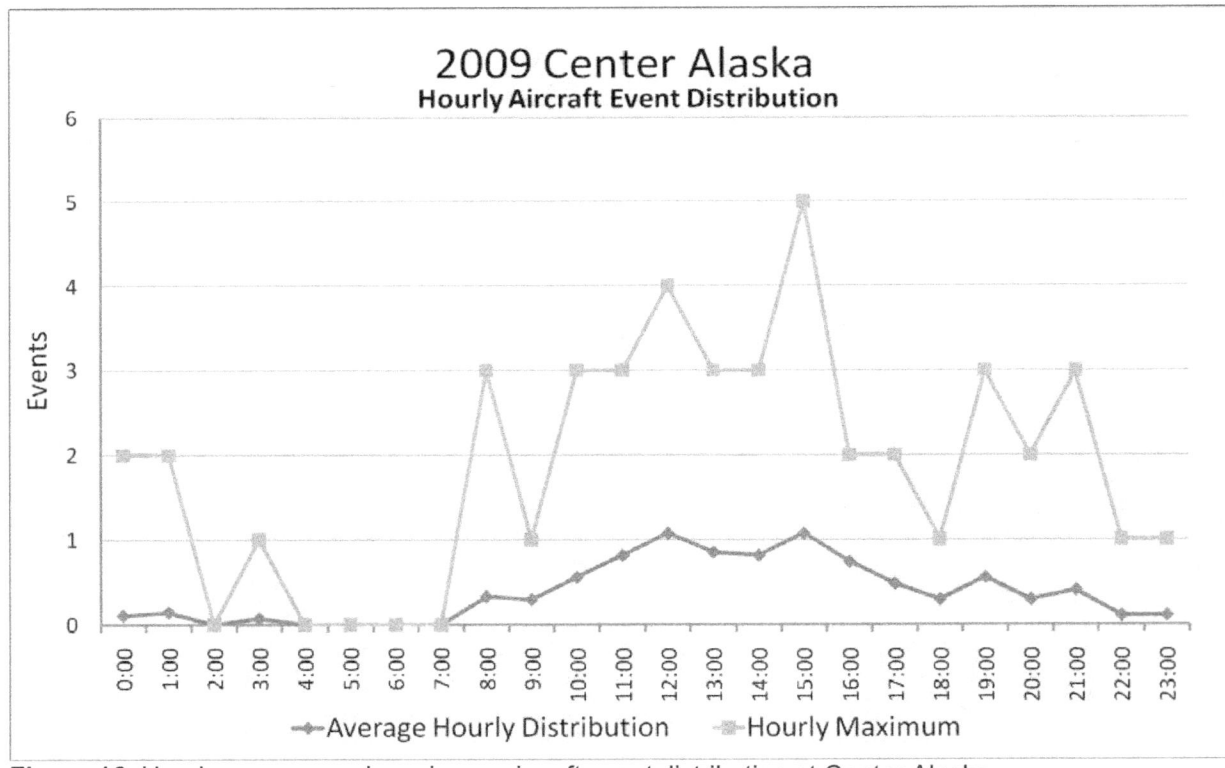

Figure 16. Hourly average and maximum aircraft event distribution at Center Alaska.

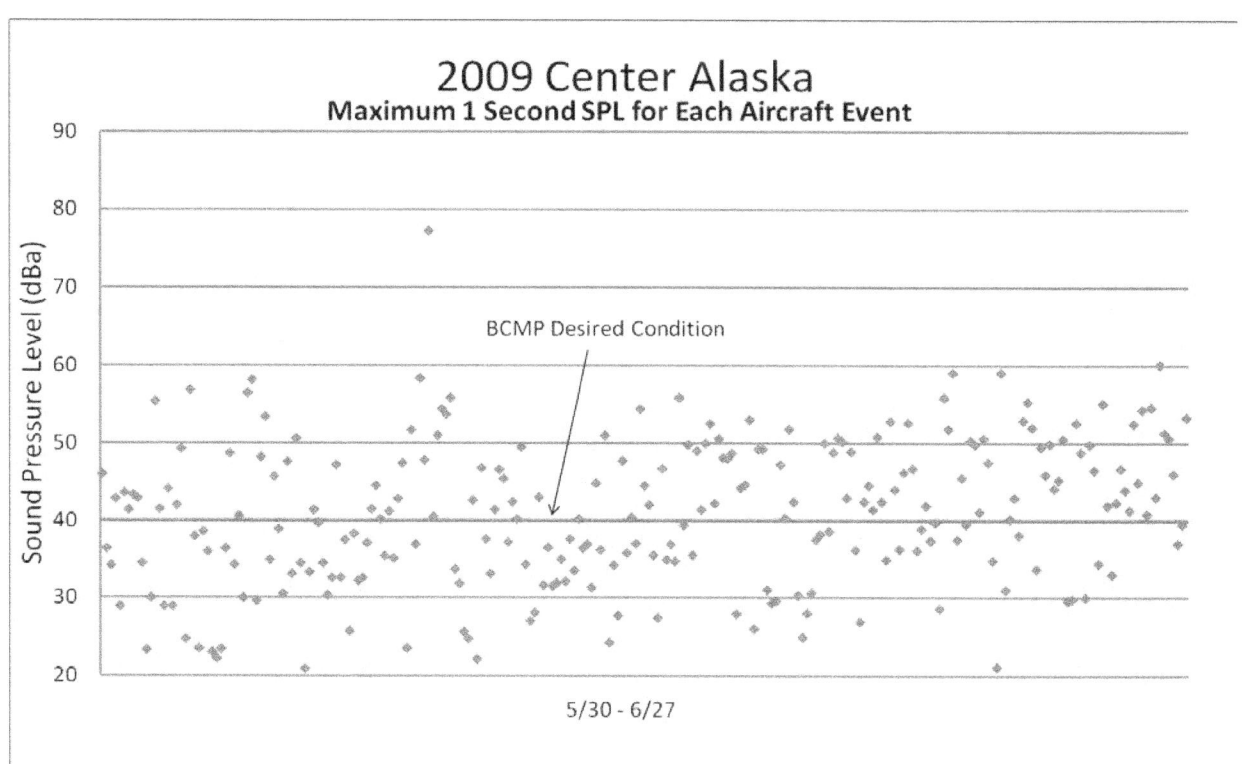

Figure 17. Maximum one-second SPL for each aircraft event identified at Center Alaska.

Dunkle Hills

Location Description: West of the Golden Zone Mine, inside the Park Boundary.

Purpose/Project: Location chosen at the request of park managers to monitor the noise impacts of over-snow vehicles inside the Denali Park Additions.

Coordinates: Lat. 63.26699, Long. 149.54153   Elevation: 828 Meters

Time at Location: 27-March-2009 – 4-April-2009

BCMP Management Zone: High   Park Ecoregion: Alpine Mountains

Access: Snowmobile

Summary: The purpose of the Dunkle Hills location was to collect data at a popular recreational snowmobiling area to provide an indication of the levels of associated noise. The Sampling site was as a New Park location and selected from locations requiring snowmobile access.

The most commonly heard sound at this site was wind (audible 75% of the time). Human made sound was audible 2.4% of the time on average. Snowmobile sound was audible 0.4% of the time on average.

Due to an error in the settings of the sound level meter (inaccurate clock), collection of SPL data was unsuccessful. As a result, only audibility analysis was performed.

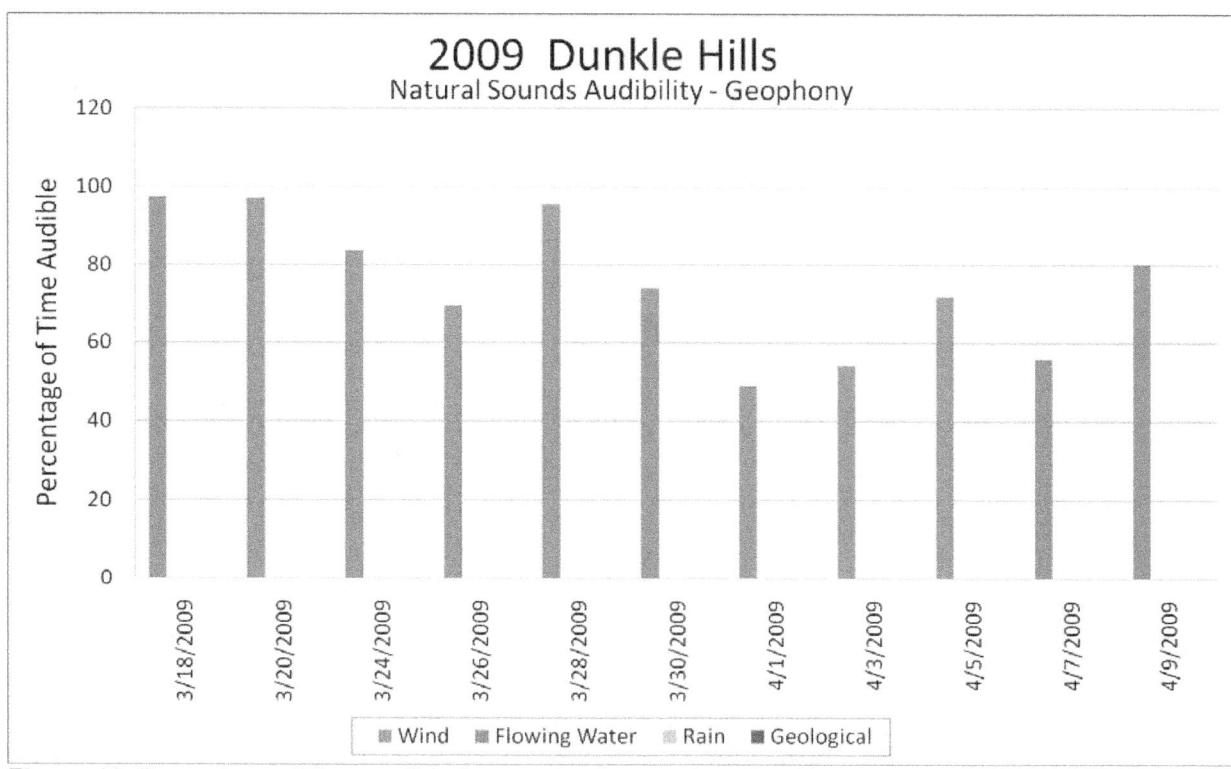

Figure 18. Percentage of time audible for geophonic sounds at Dunkle Hills.

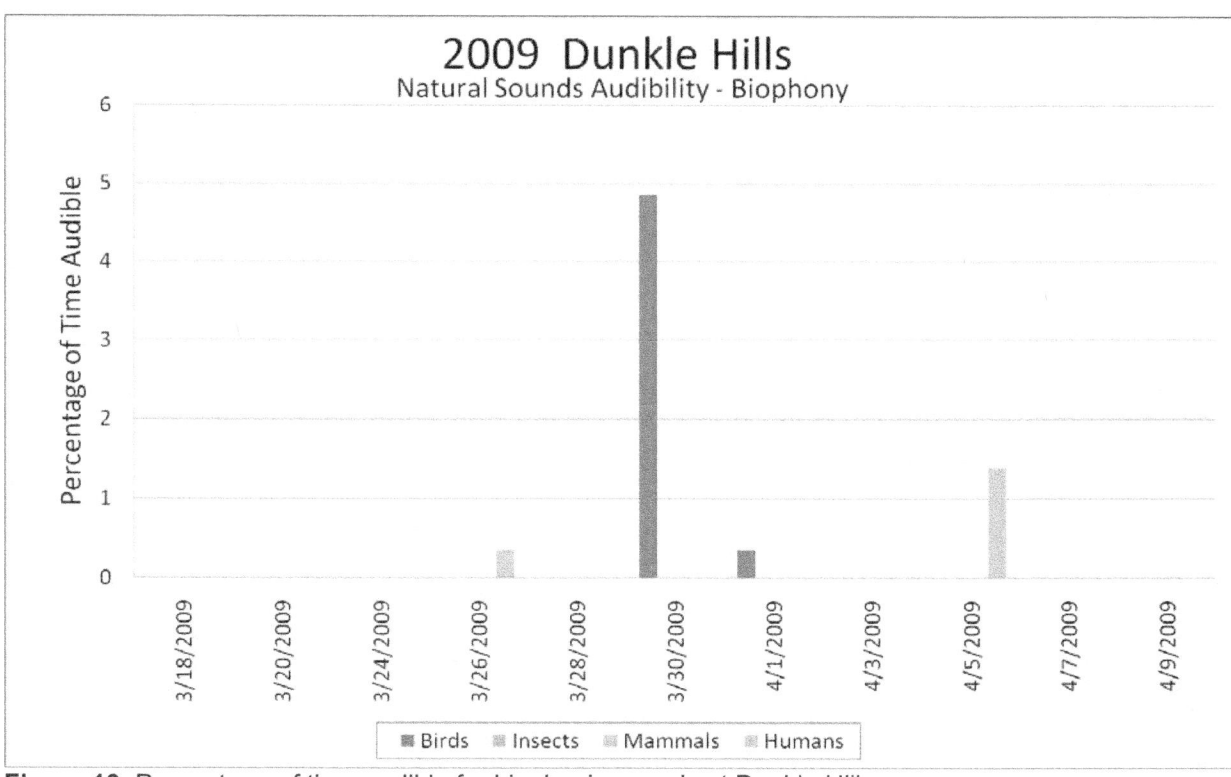

Figure 19. Percentage of time audible for biophonic sounds at Dunkle Hills.

21

Herron River

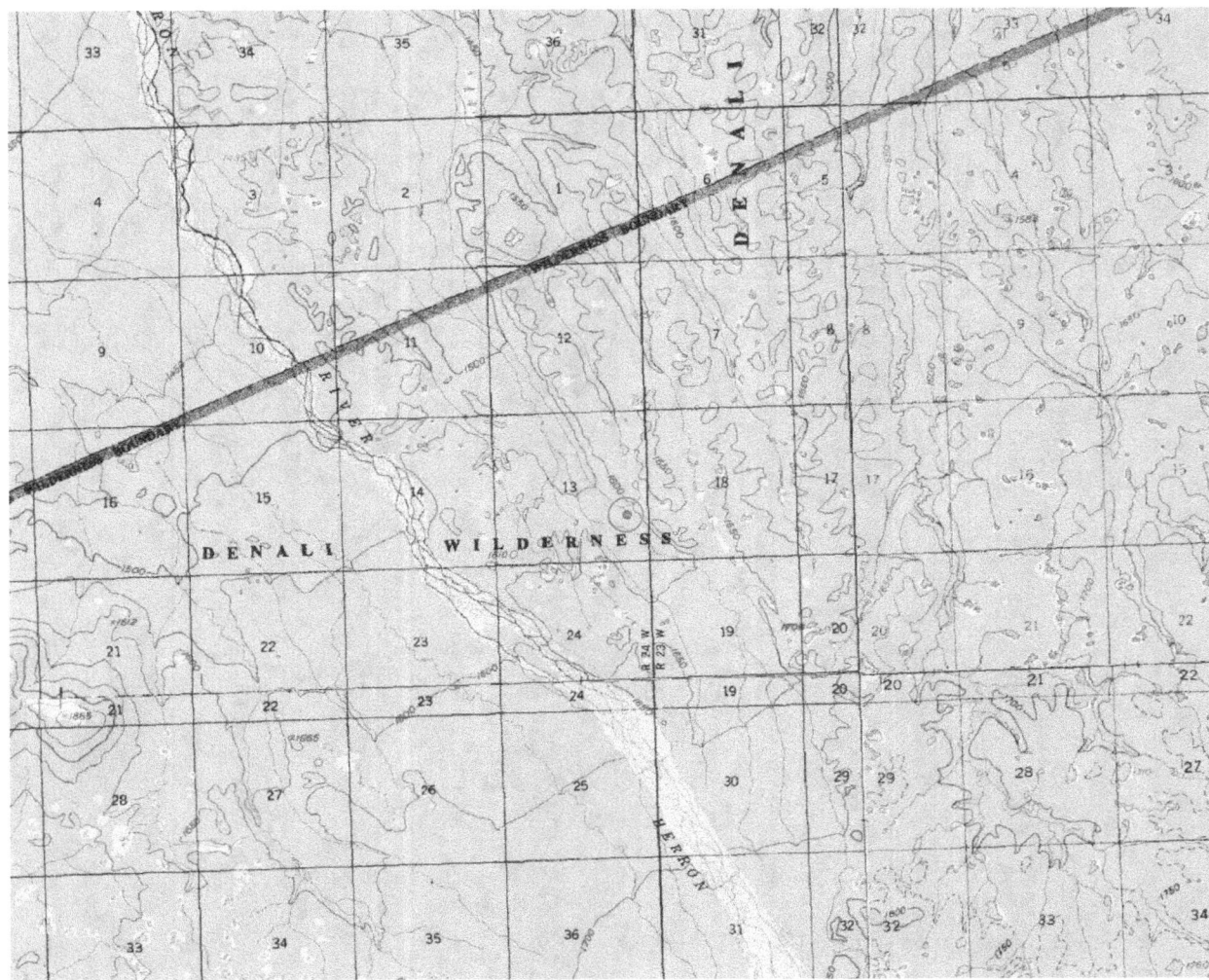

Location Description: At the confluence of the Eldridge and an unnamed glacier ~2 Km West of the Park Boundary.

Purpose/Project: Location randomly chosen from the LTEM grid as part of the long-term Denali Soundscape inventorying and monitoring sampling plan.

Coordinates: Lat. 63.05045, Long. 150.07388   Elevation: 893 Meters

Time at Location: Jun-01 to Aug-01, 2007

BCMP Management Zone: Medium   Park Ecoregion: Nonvegetated Alpine Mountains

Access: Helicopter

Summary: The purpose of the Herron River location was to collect data at one of the long-term ecological monitoring (LTEM) grid points, as outlined in the above sampling plan. LTEM grid point #113 was stratified as an Old Park (Wilderness) location and randomly selected from all locations requiring aircraft access.

The most commonly heard sounds at this site were birds (audible 42% of the time), wind (24%), and insects (6%). Human made sound was audible 1.2% of the time on average. Conditions exceeded the BCMP percent audible standard 8% of the time, number of events per day 57% of the time, and maximum SPL 31% of the time.

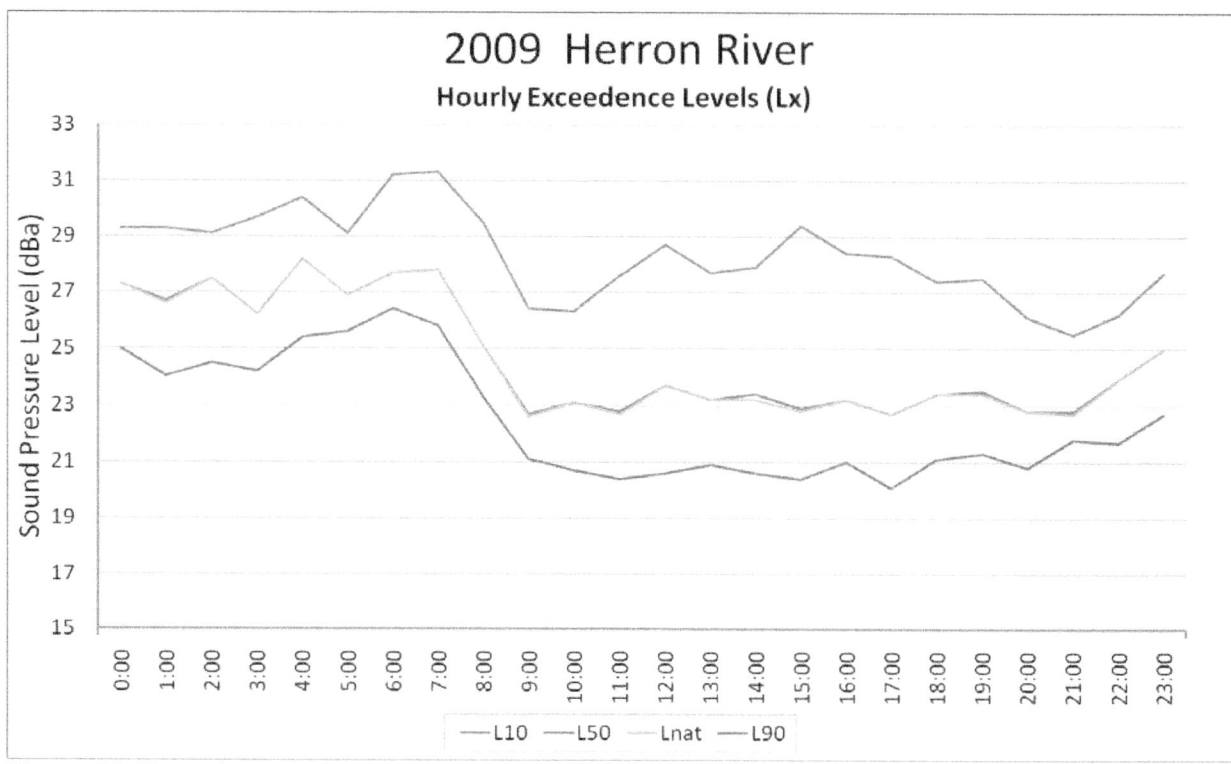

Figure 20. Exceedence levels for Herron River.

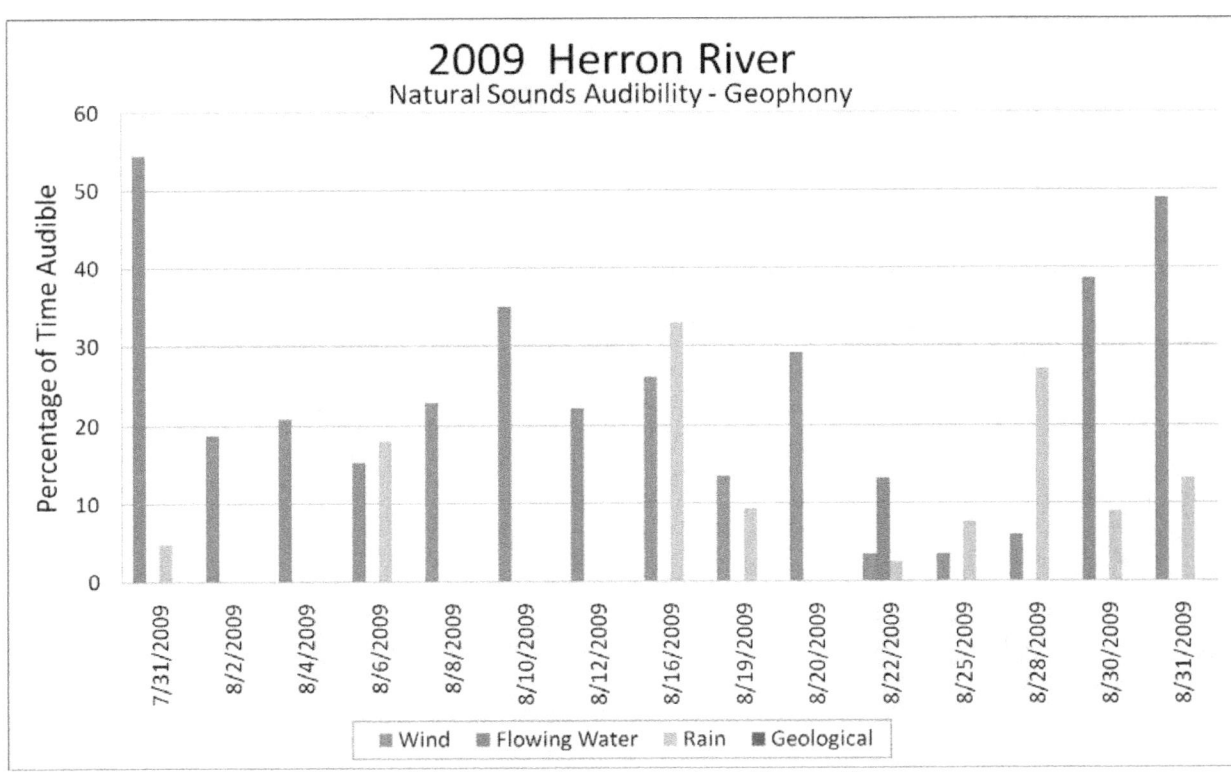

Figure 21. Percentage of time audible for geophonic sounds at Herron River.

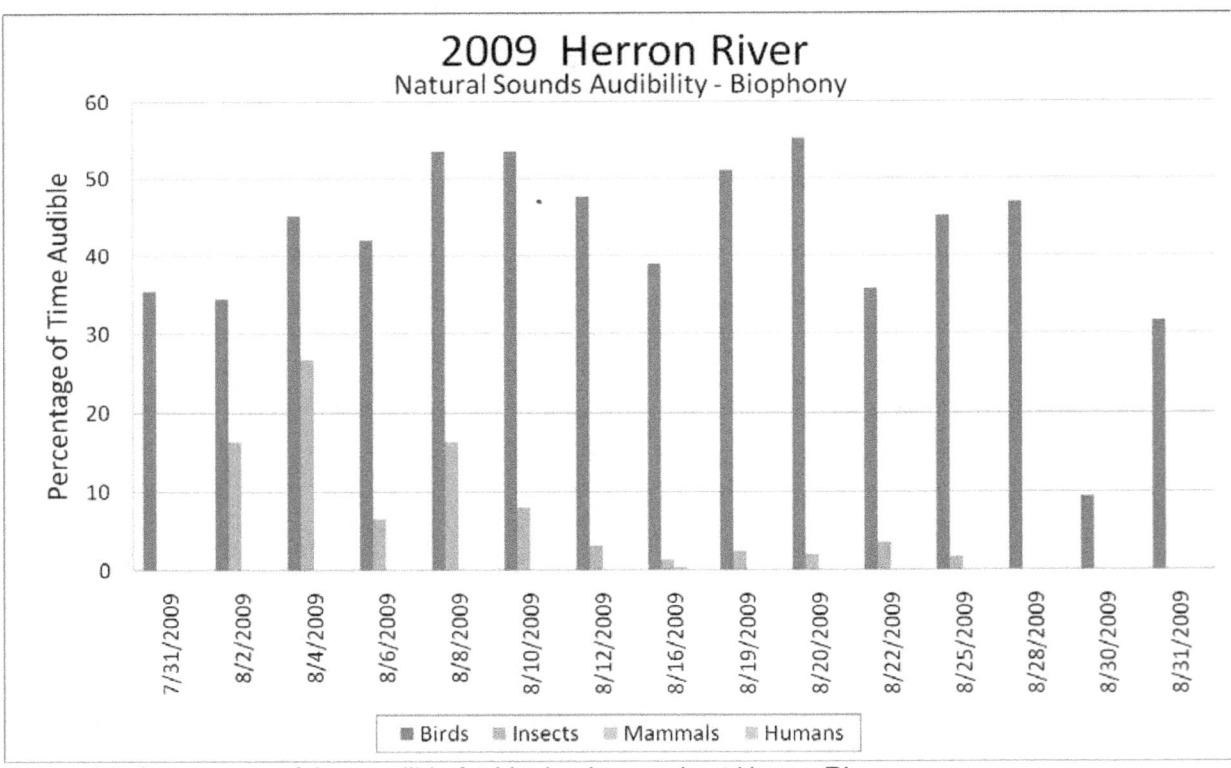

Figure 22. Percentage of time audible for biophonic sounds at Herron River.

24

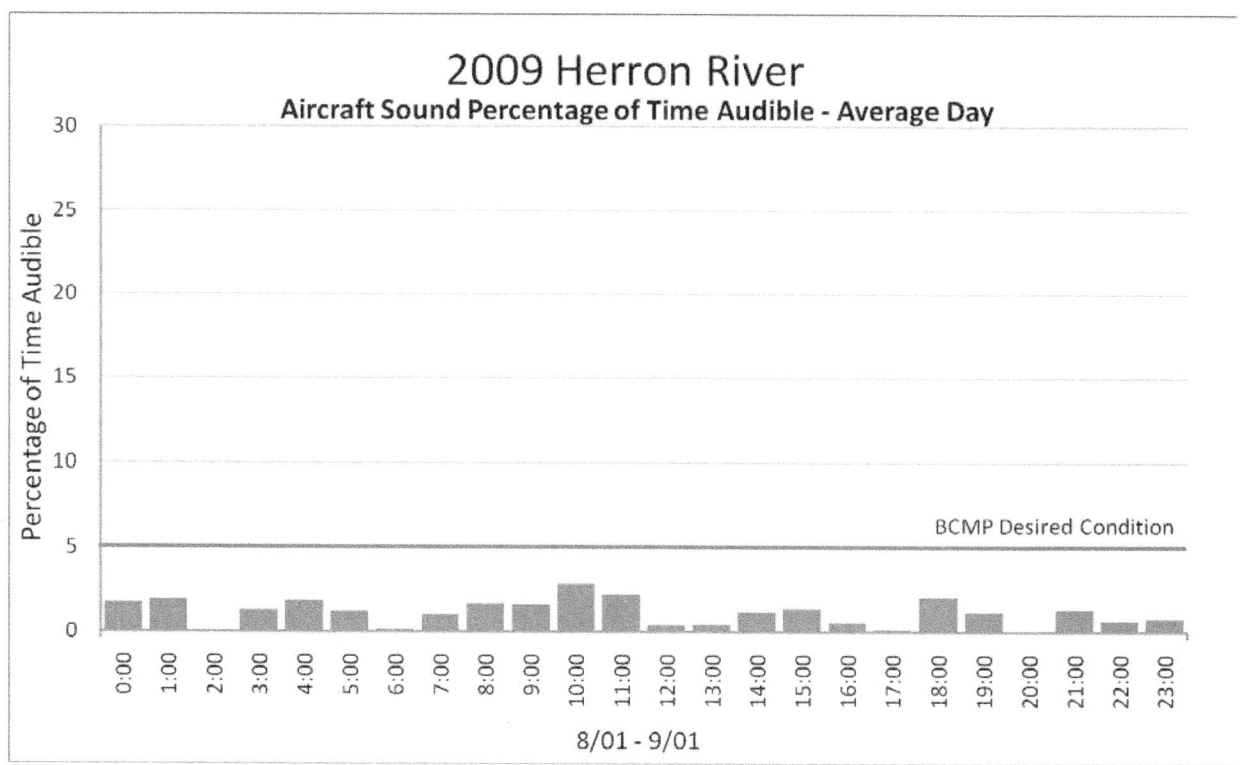

Figure 23. Audibility of aircraft noise for an average day, by hour, at Herron River.

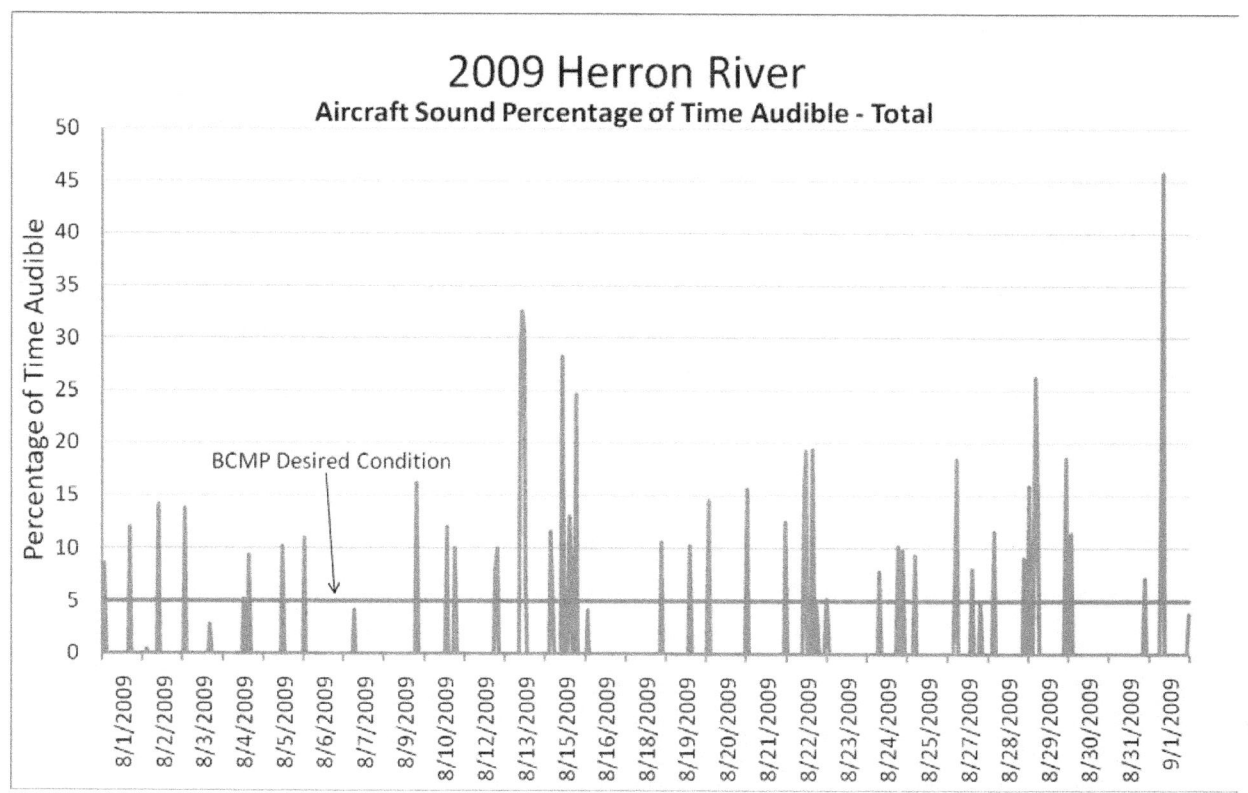

Figure 24. Audibility of aircraft noise at Herron River.

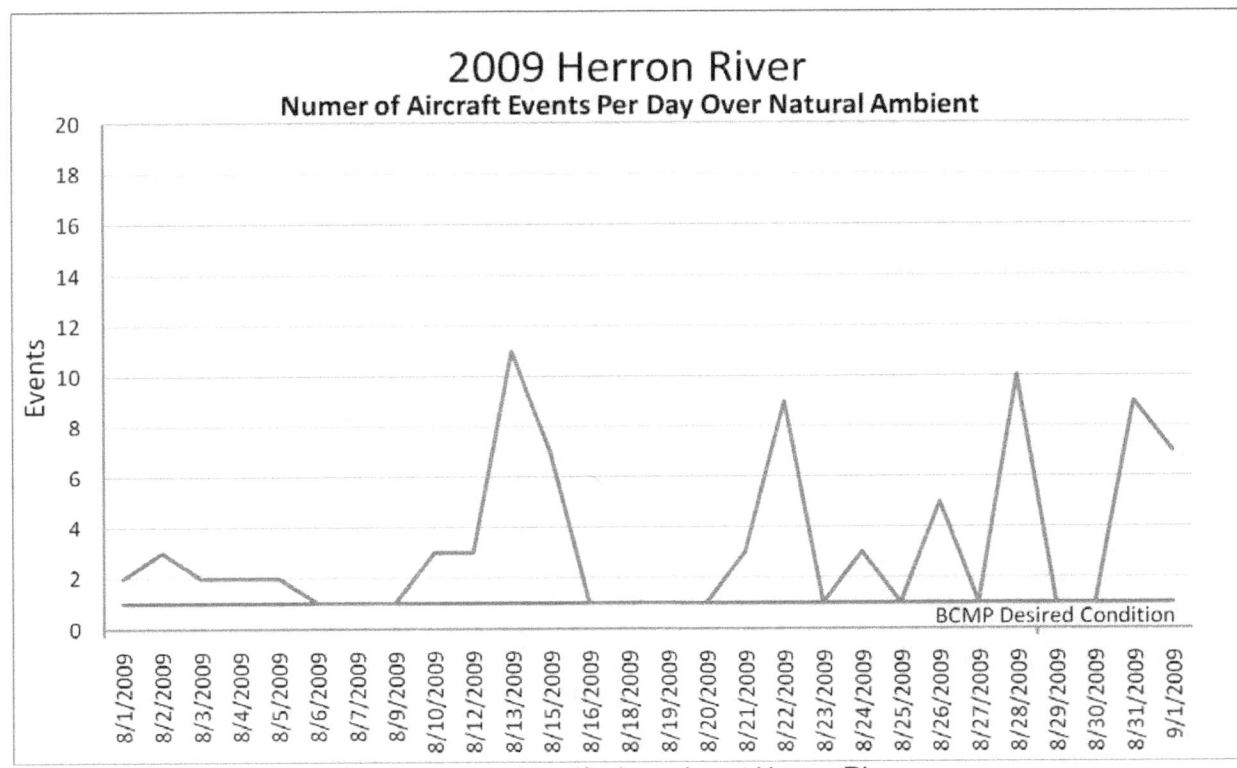

Figure 25. Number of aircraft noise events identified per day at Herron River.

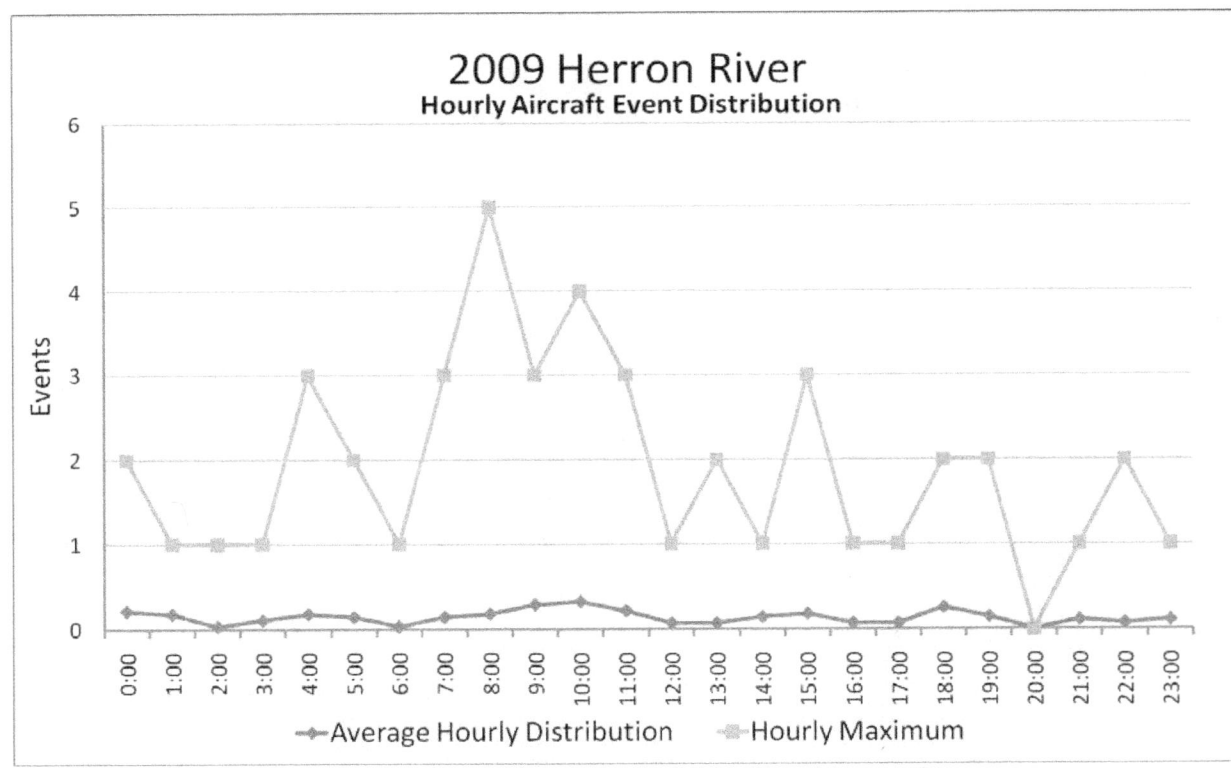

Figure 26. Hourly average and maximum aircraft event distribution at Herron River.

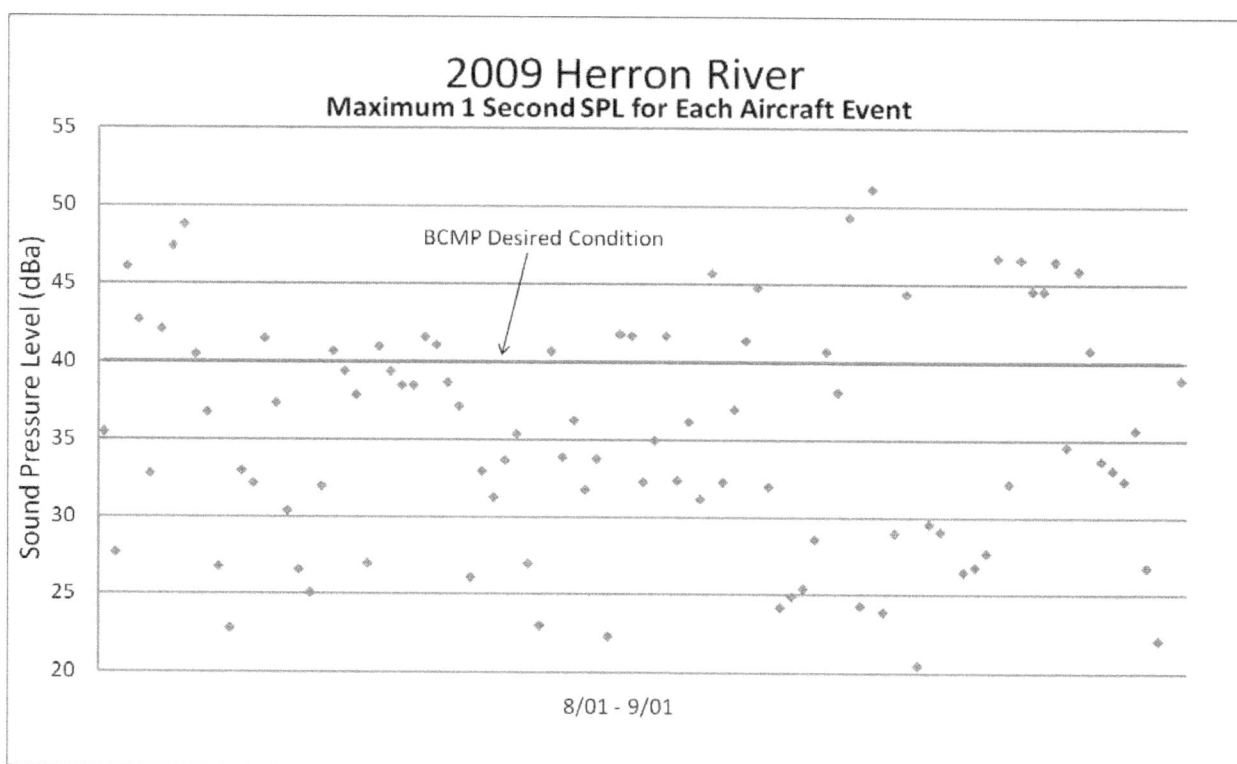

Figure 27. Maximum one-second SPL for each aircraft event identified at Herron River.

Lower Slippery Creek

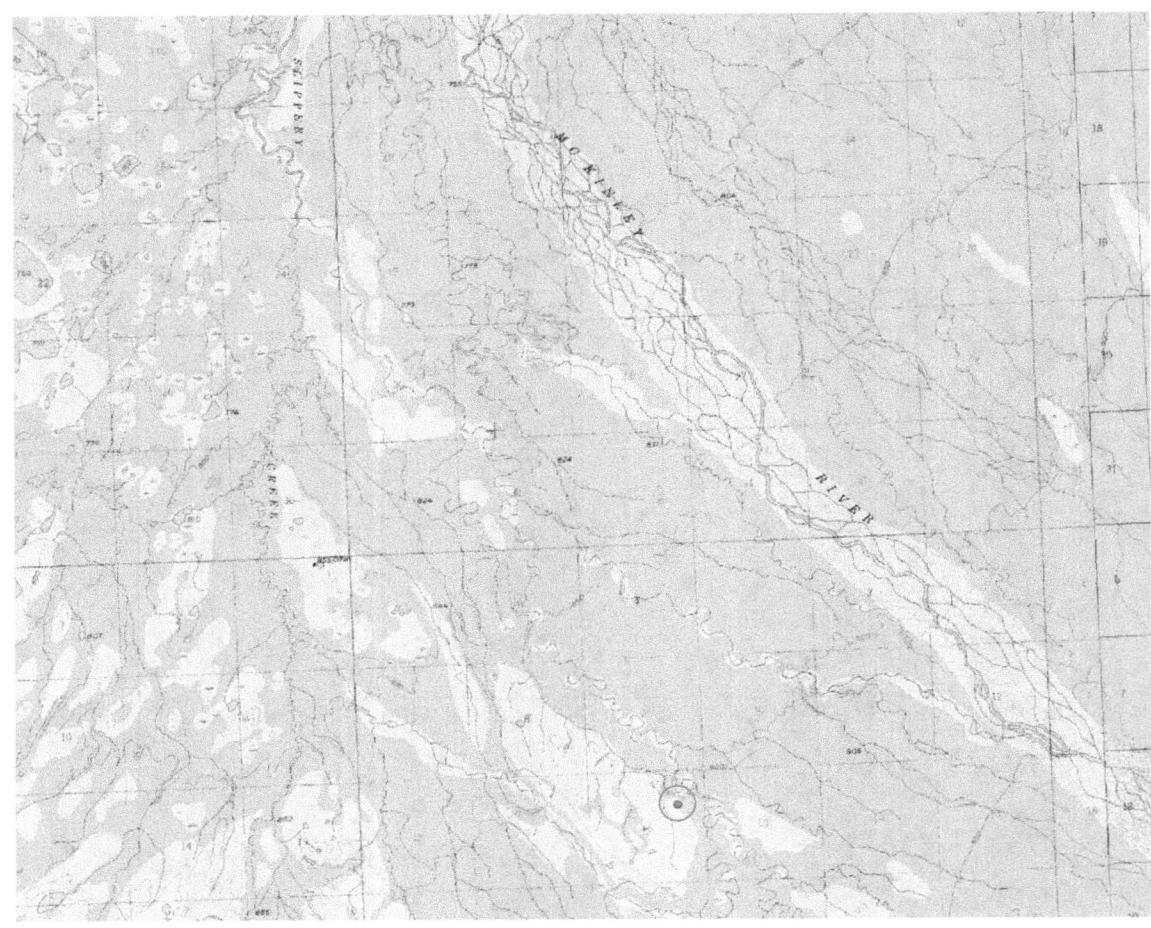

Location Description: Slippery Creek ~37 Km Southeast of Lake Minchumina.

Purpose/Project: Location randomly chosen from the LTEM grid as part of the long-term Denali
Soundscape inventorying and monitoring sampling plan.

Coordinates: Lat. 63.62359, Long. 151.24017   Elevation: 365 Meters

Time at Location: 20-July-2009 – 16-Sept-2009

BCMP Management Zone: Low   Park Ecoregion: Eolian Lowlands

Access: Helicopter

Summary: The purpose of the Lower Slippery Creek location was to collect data at one of the
long-term ecological monitoring (LTEM) grid points as outlined in the above sampling plan.
LTEM grid point #187 was stratified as a New Park location and randomly selected from all
locations requiring aircraft access.

The most commonly heard sounds at this site were birds (audible 31% of the time), insects
(18%), and wind (14%). Human made sound was audible 2.2% of the time on average.
Conditions exceeded the BCMP percent audible standard 18% of the time, number of events per
day 94% of the time, and maximum SPL 19% of the time.

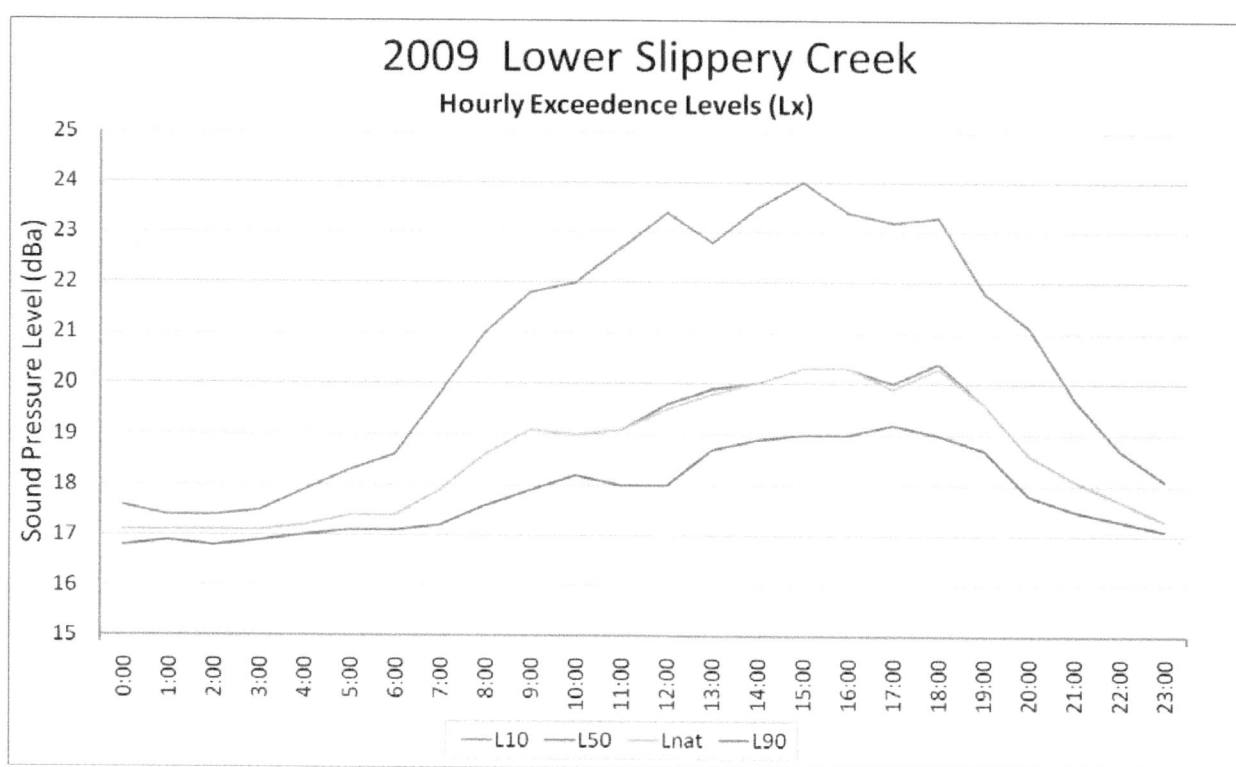

Figure 28. Exceedence levels for Lower Slippery Creek.

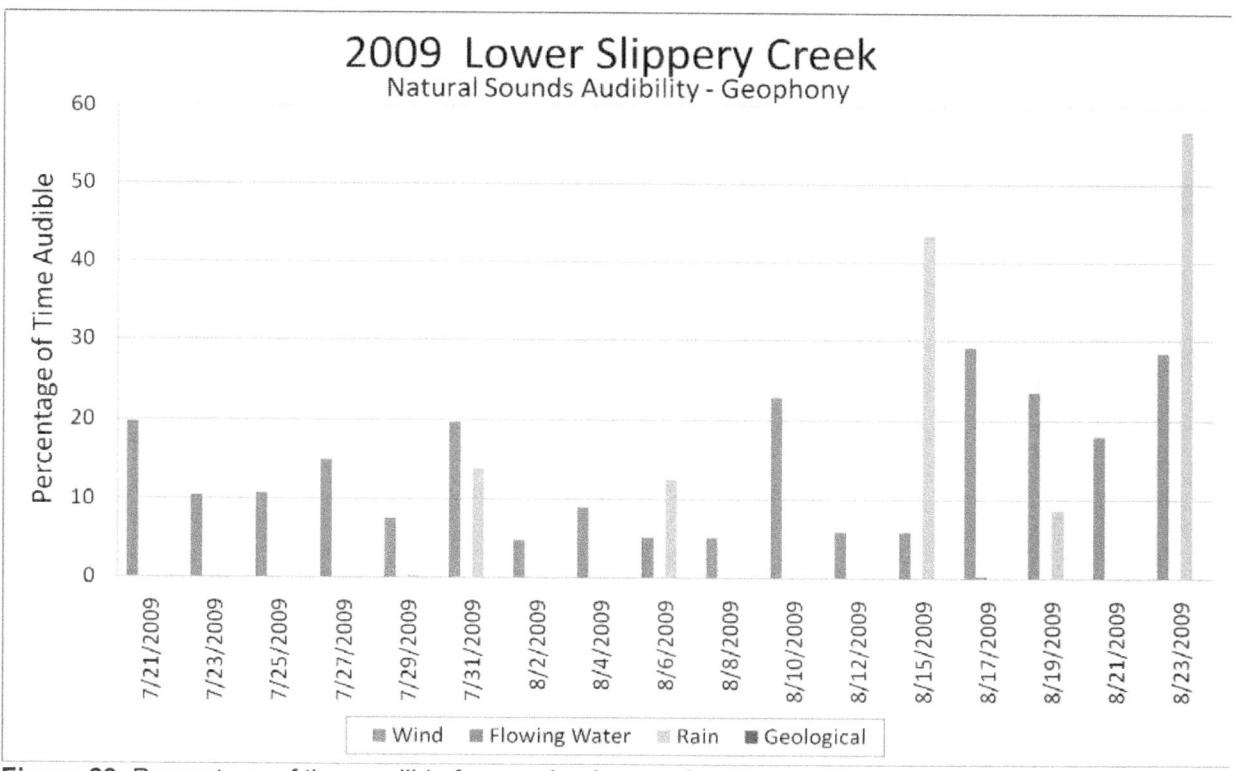

Figure 29. Percentage of time audible for geophonic sounds at Lower Slippery Creek.

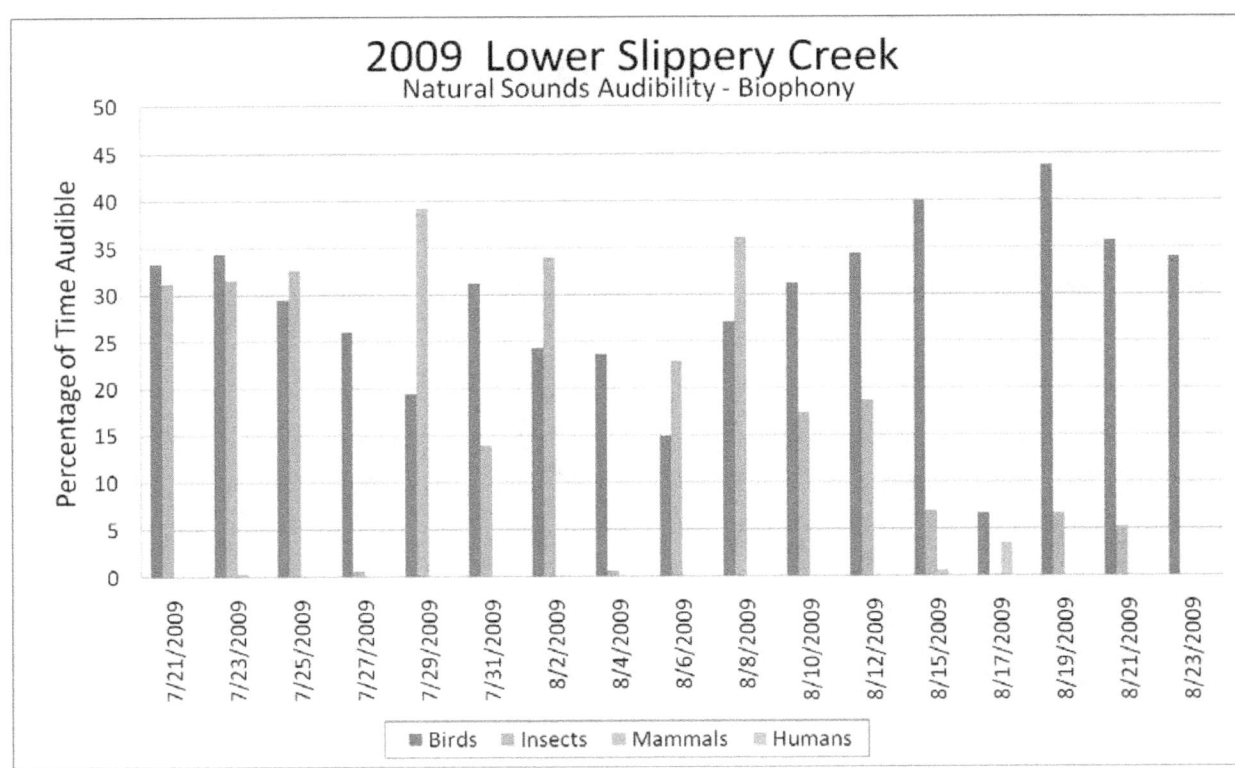

Figure 30. Percentage of time audible for biophonic sounds at Lower Slippery Creek.

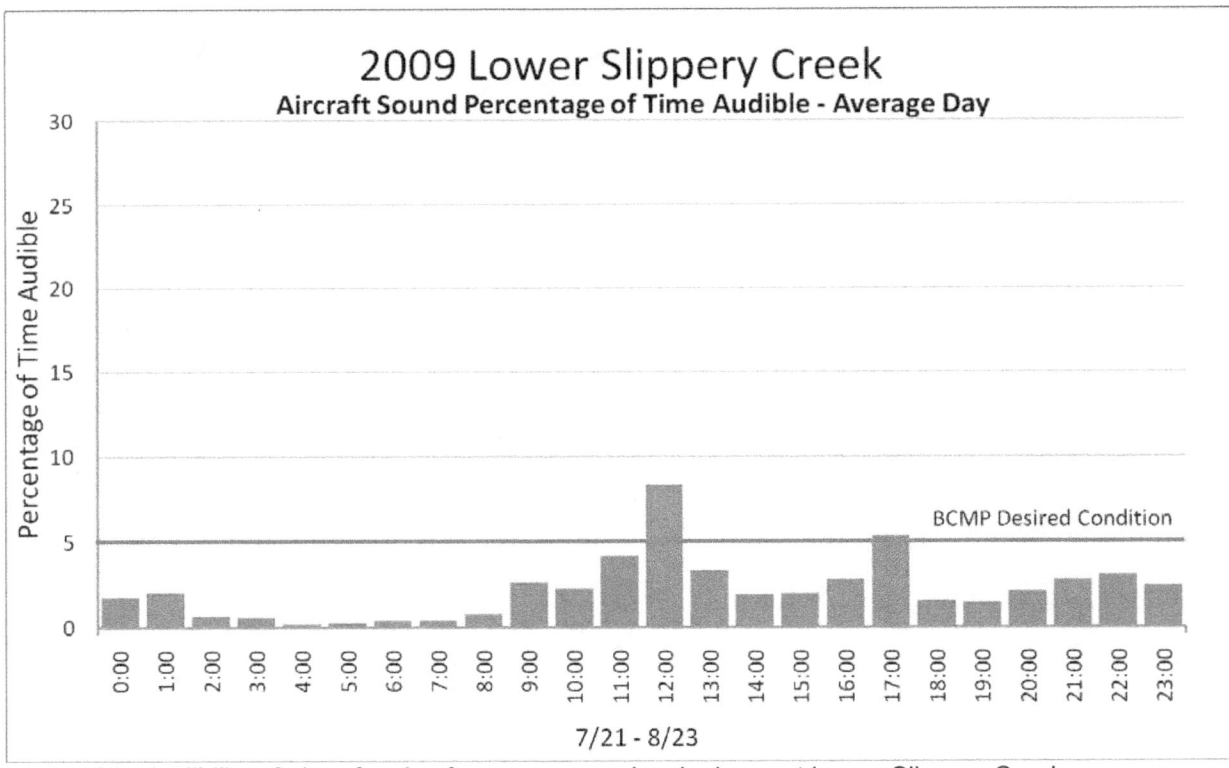

Figure 31. Audibility of aircraft noise for an average day, by hour, at Lower Slippery Creek.

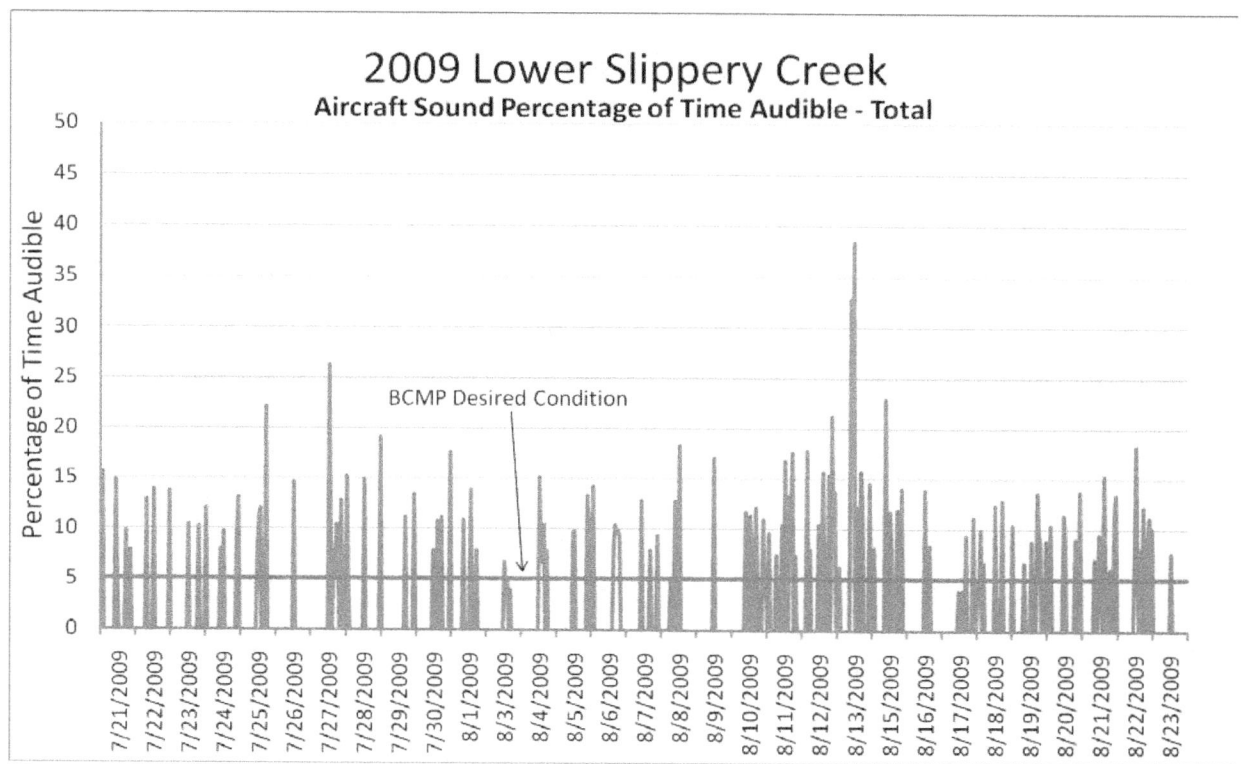

Figure 32. Audibility of aircraft noise at Lower Slippery Creek.

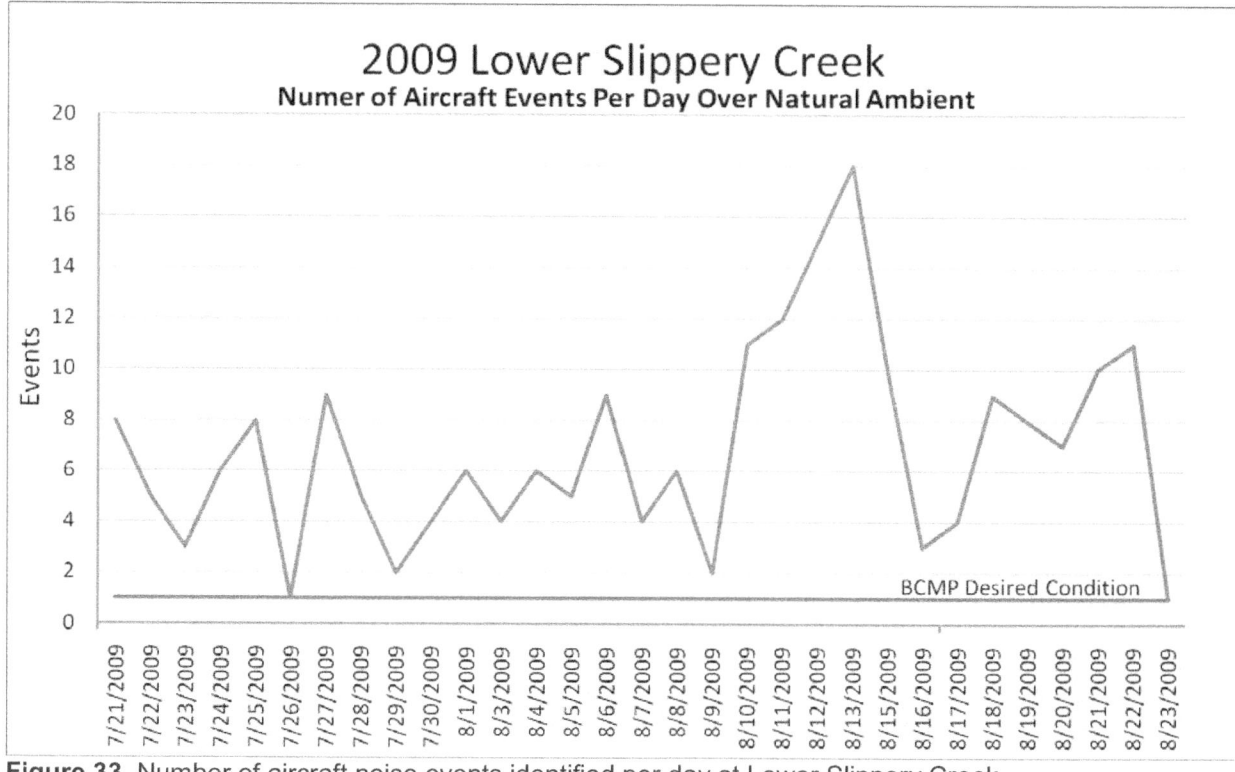

Figure 33. Number of aircraft noise events identified per day at Lower Slippery Creek.

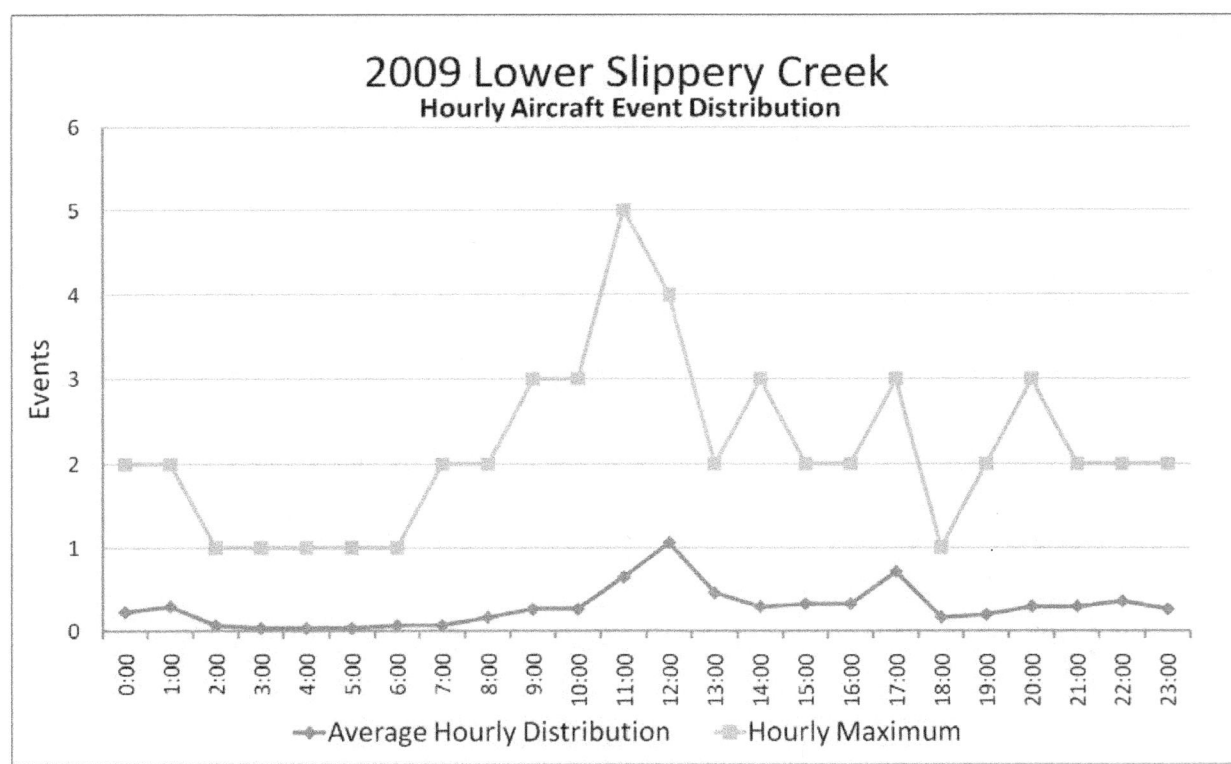

Figure 34. Hourly average and maximum aircraft event distribution at Lower Slippery Creek.

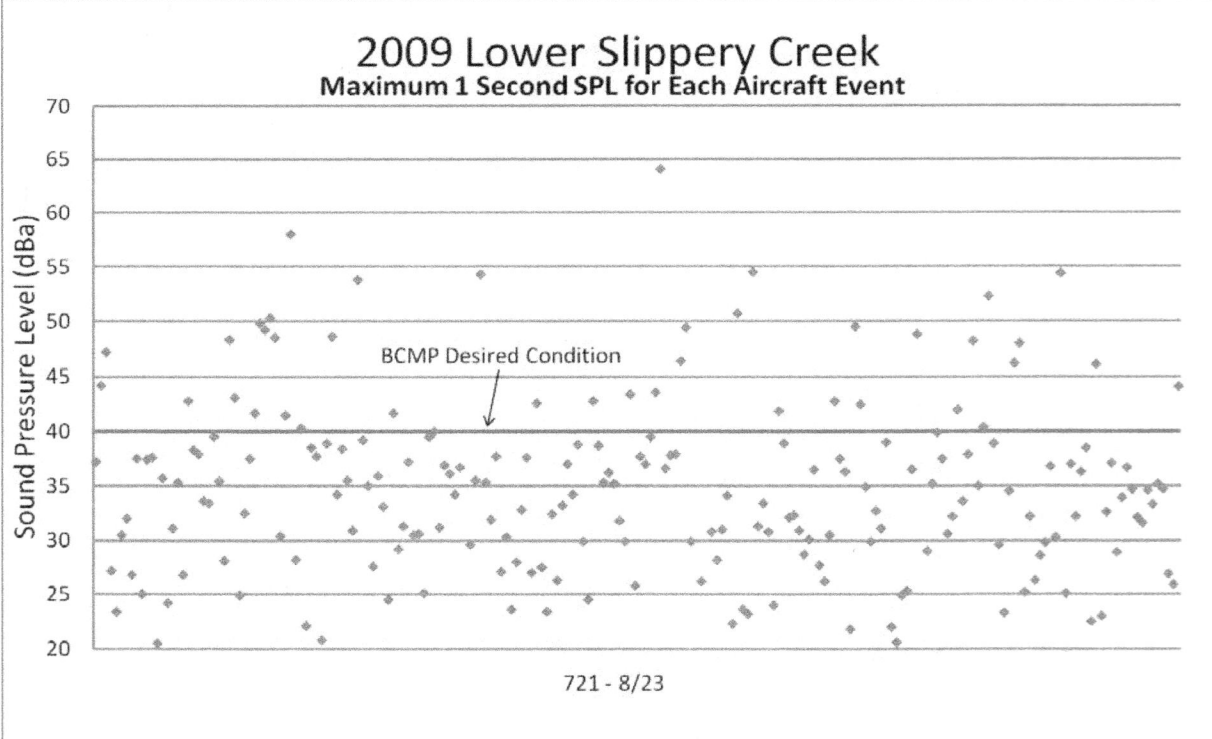

Figure 35. Maximum one-second SPL for each aircraft event identified at Lower Slippery Creek.

32

Triple Lakes

Location Description: Adjacent to the triple lakes trail, half way between the two bigger lakes.

Purpose/Project: Location of interest chosen at the request of park management to assess the impacts from overflight noise in this highly visited area.

Coordinates: Lat. 63.66258, Long. 148.87473   Elevation: 654 Meters

Time at Location: 30-June-2009 – 6-August-2009

BCMP Management Zone: Low   Park Ecoregion: Boreal Mountains

Access: Foot

Summary: The purpose of the Triple Lakes location was to collect acoustic data at this popular Wilderness day-hiking area. Park managers are concerned at the possibility that hikers may be experiencing high levels of aircraft noise exposure.

The most commonly heard sounds at this site were birds (audible 42% of the time), wind (19%), insects (9%), and rain (5%). Human made sound was audible 11.0% of the time on average. Conditions exceeded the BCMP percent audible standard 65% of the time, number of events per day 100% of the time, and maximum SPL 64% of the time.

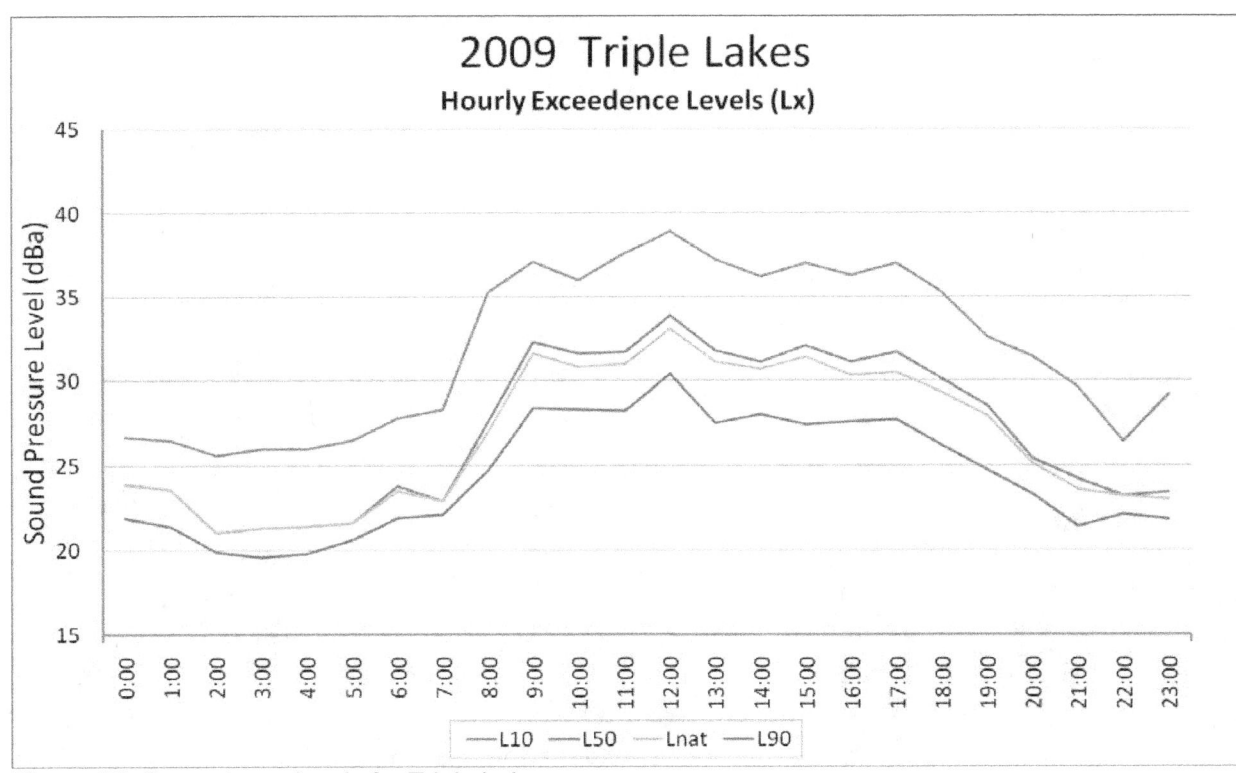

Figure 36. Exceedence levels for Triple Lakes.

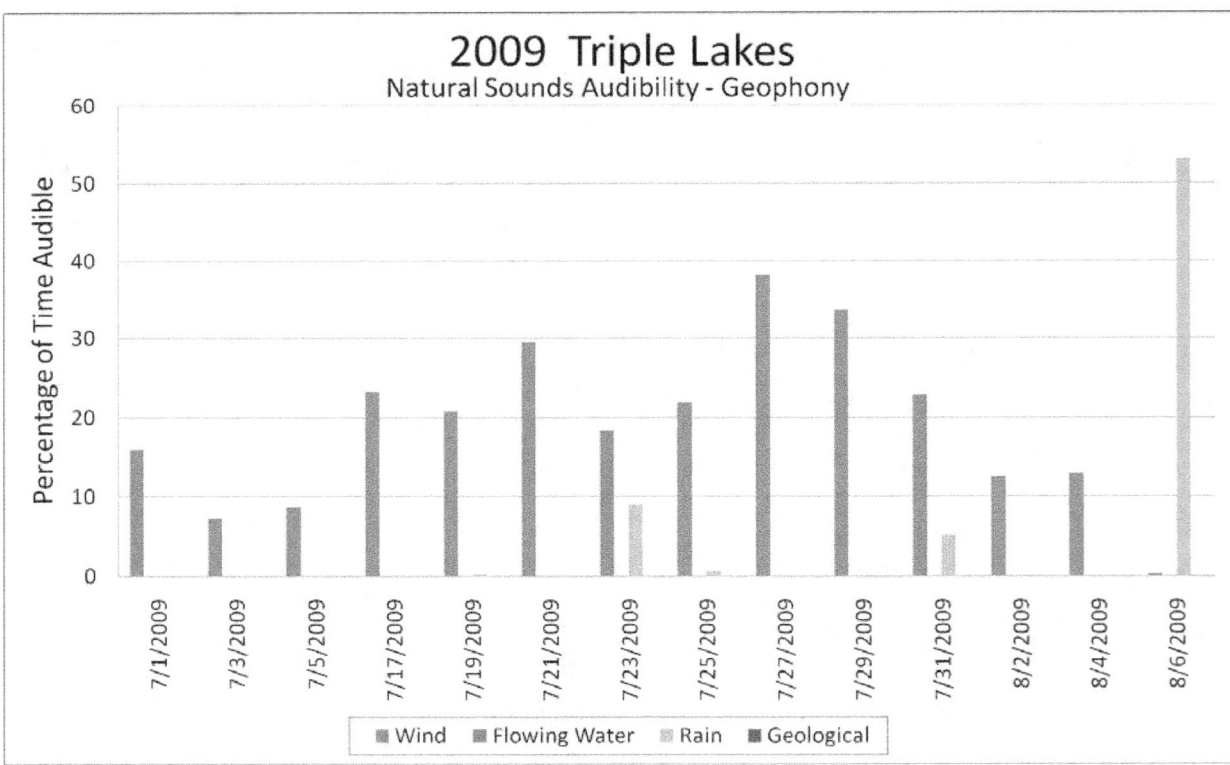

Figure 37. Percentage of time audible for geophonic sounds at Triple Lakes.

34

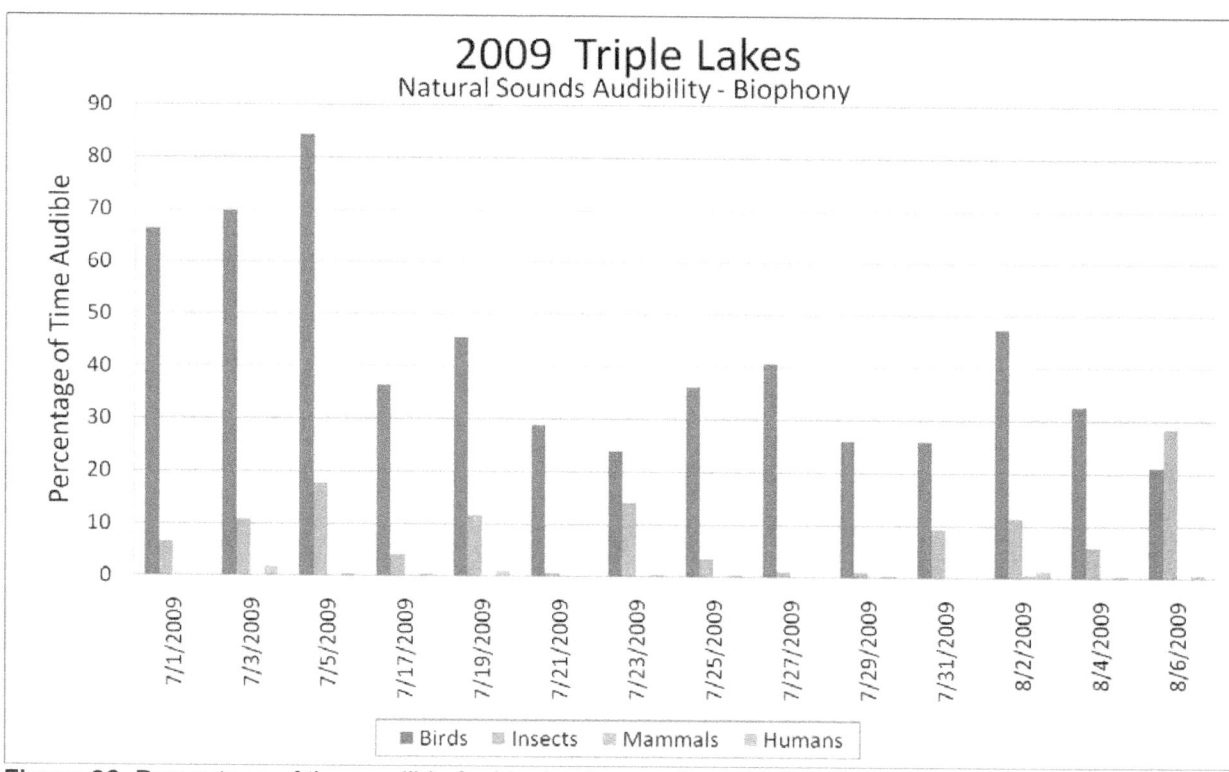

Figure 38. Percentage of time audible for biophonic sounds at Triple Lakes.

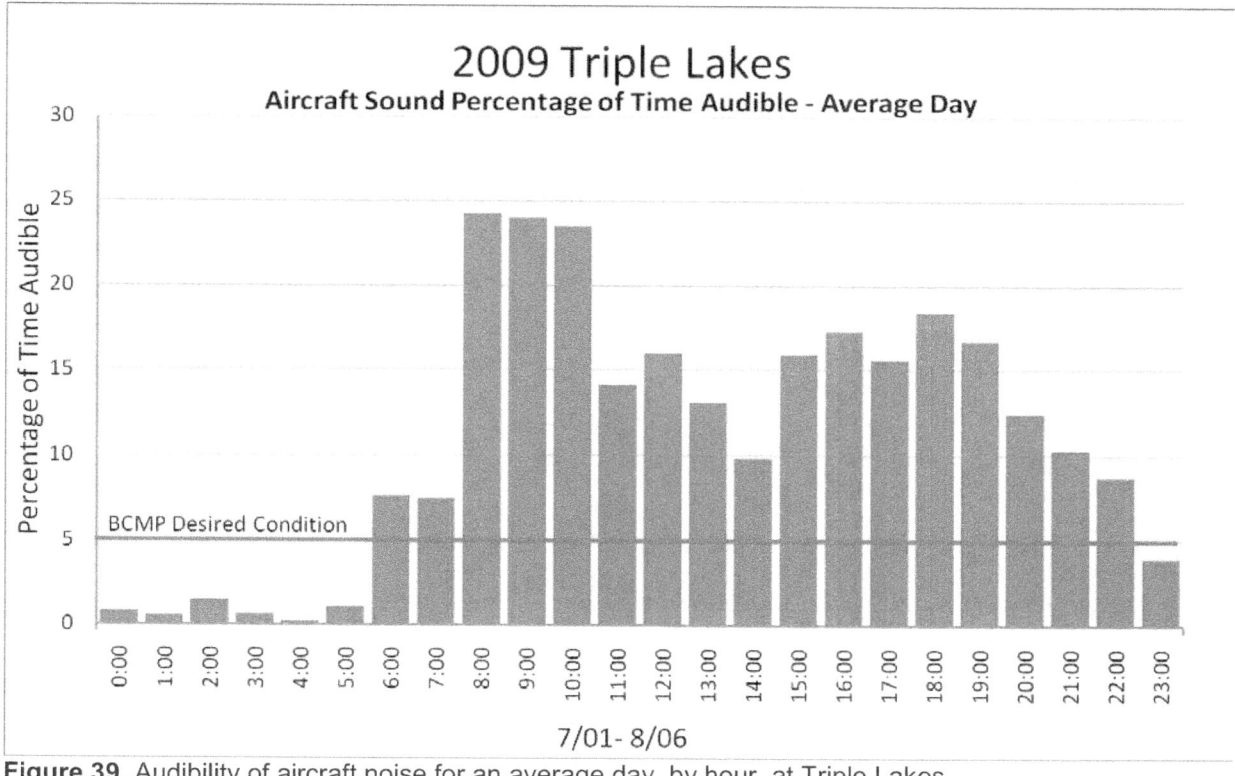

Figure 39. Audibility of aircraft noise for an average day, by hour, at Triple Lakes.

35

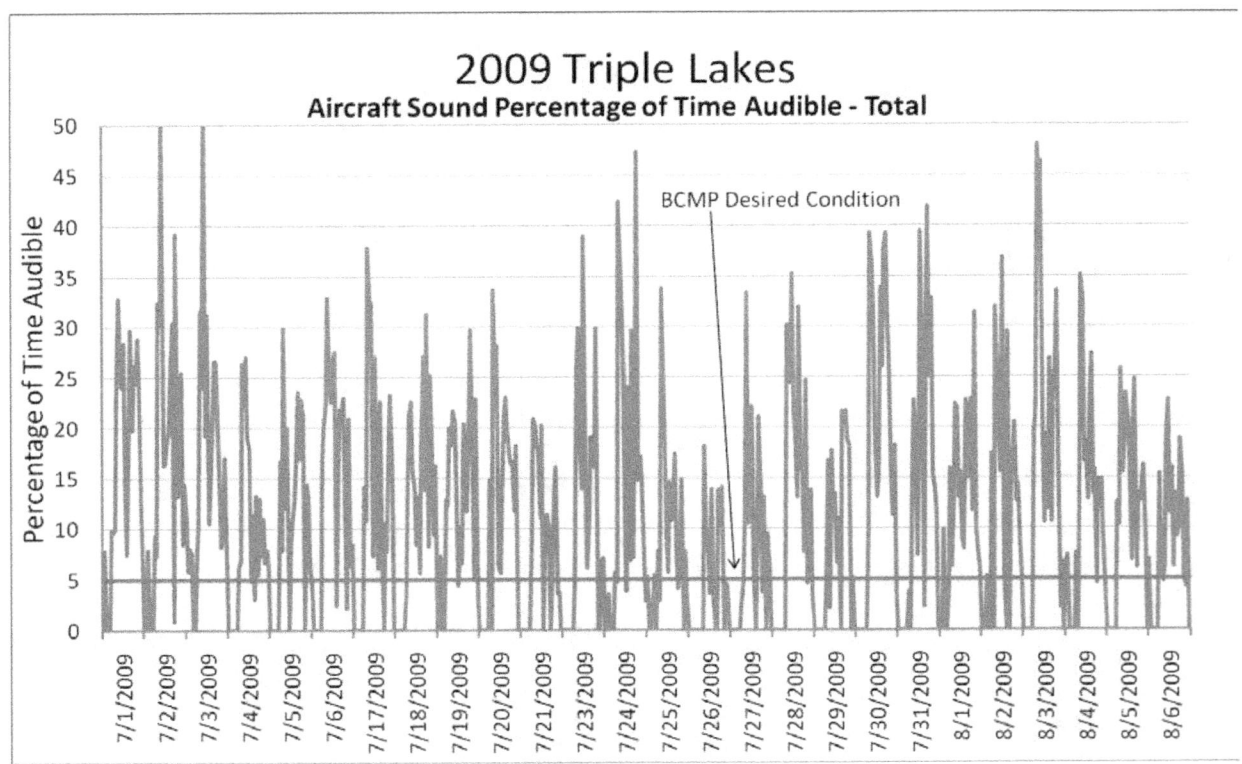

Figure 40. Audibility of aircraft noise at Triple Lakes.

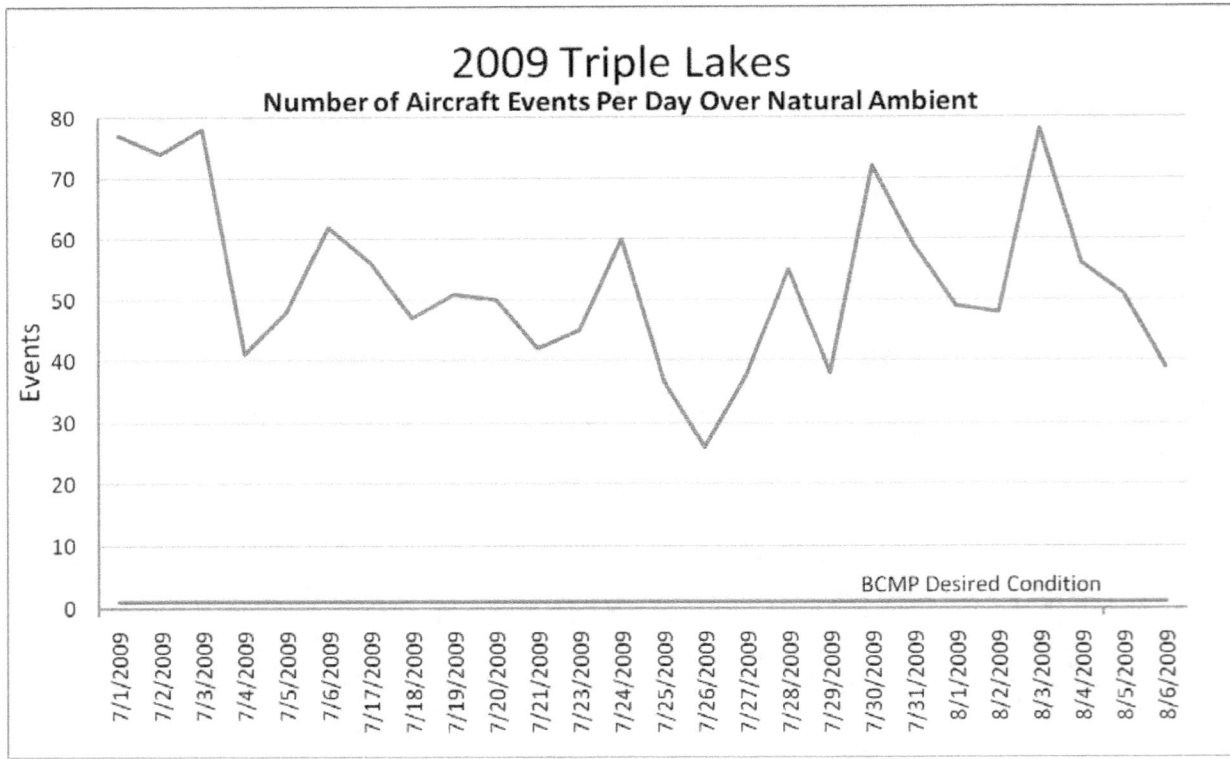

Figure 41. Number of aircraft noise events identified per day at Triple Lakes.

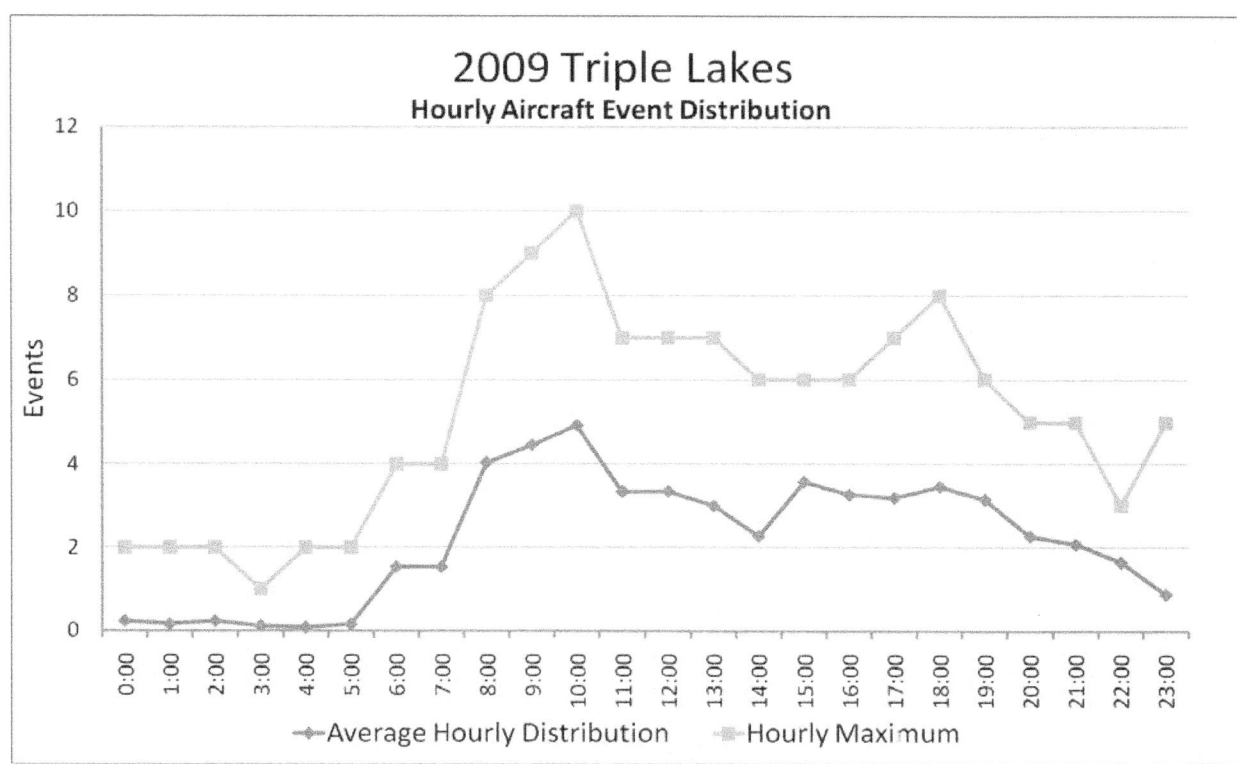

Figure 42. Hourly average and maximum aircraft event distribution at Triple Lakes.

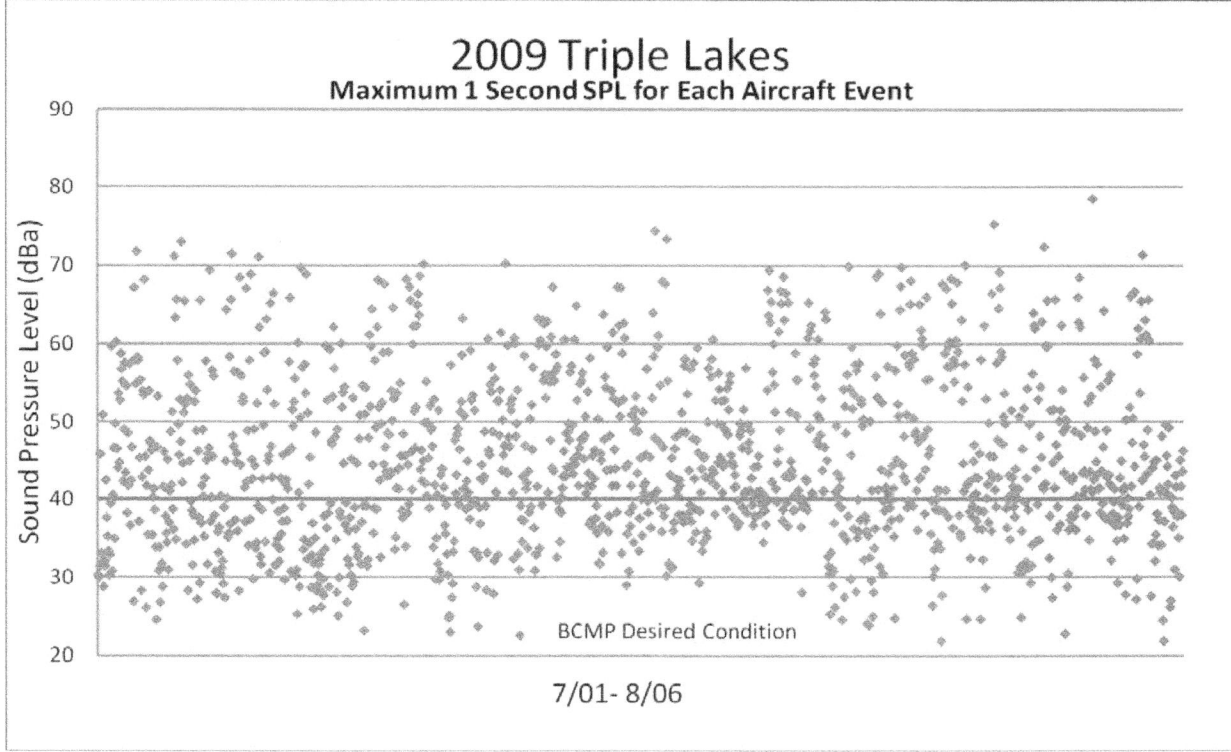

Figure 43. Maximum one-second SPL for each aircraft event identified at Triple Lakes.

Upper Tokositna Glacier

Location Description: At the culmination of the medial moraine at the fork in the upper Tokositna Glacier.

Purpose/Project: Location randomly chosen from the LTEM grid as part of the long-term Denali Soundscape inventorying and monitoring sampling plan.

Coordinates: Lat. 62.88184, Long. 150.88486   Elevation: 1025 Meters

Time at Location: 17-August-2009 – 15-Sept-2009

BCMP Management Zone: Very High   Park Ecoregion: Nonvegetated Alpine Mountains

Access: Helicopter

Summary: The purpose of the Upper Tokositna Galcier location was to collect data at one of the long-term ecological monitoring (LTEM) grid points as outlined in the above sampling plan. LTEM grid point #57 was stratified as a New Park location and randomly selected from all locations requiring aircraft access.

Collection of audibility data at this site was not successful, so no audibility analysis is possible. However, SPL data was collected, so a visual analysis of human-caused noise and BCMP indicator analysis was performed.

Human made sound was audible 6.2% of the time on average. Conditions exceeded the BCMP percent audible standard 0% of the time, number of events per day 7% of the time, and maximum SPL 15% of the time.

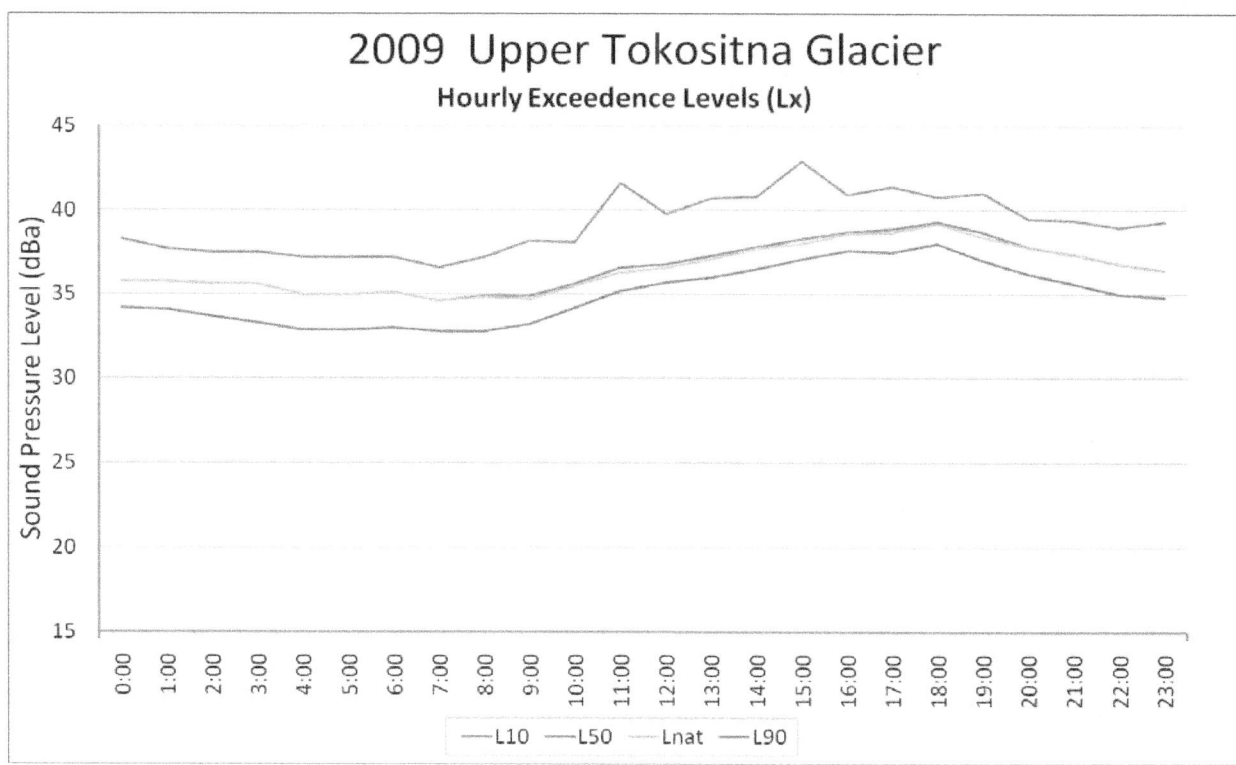

Figure 44. Exceedence levels for Upper Tokositna Glacier.

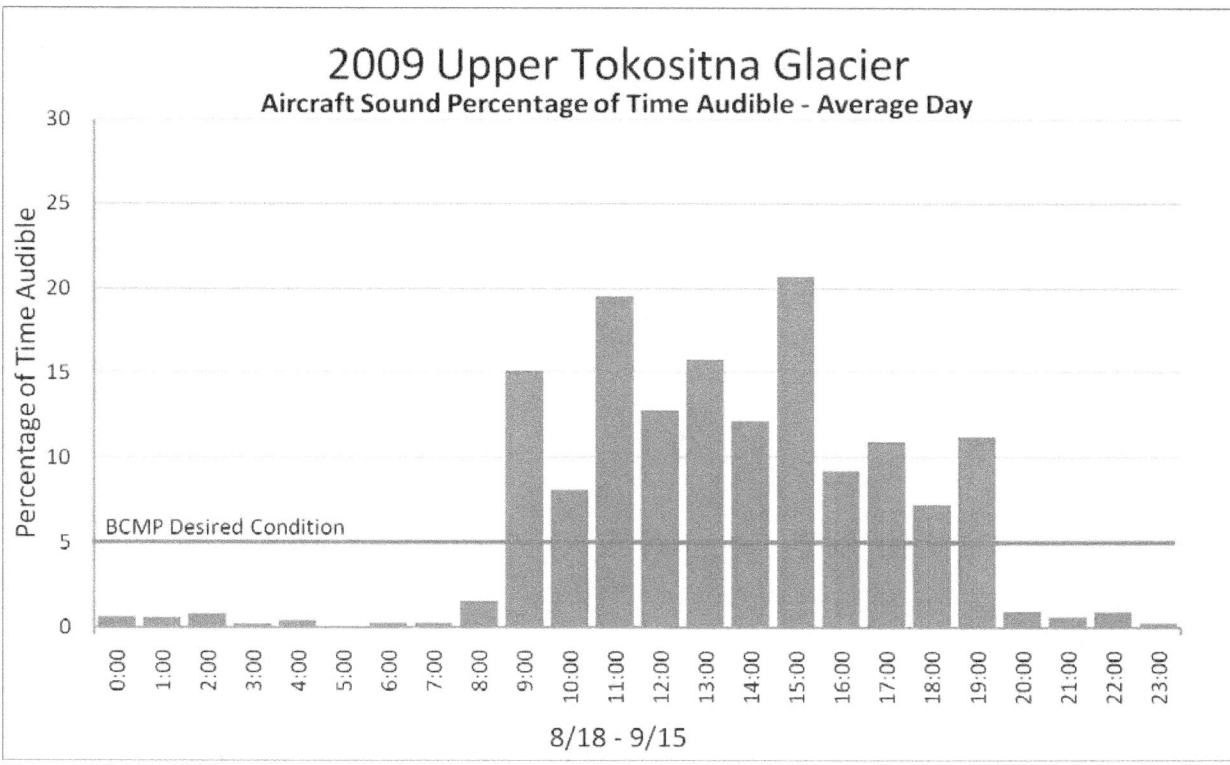

Figure 45. Audibility of aircraft noise for an average day, by hour, at Upper Tokositna Glacier.

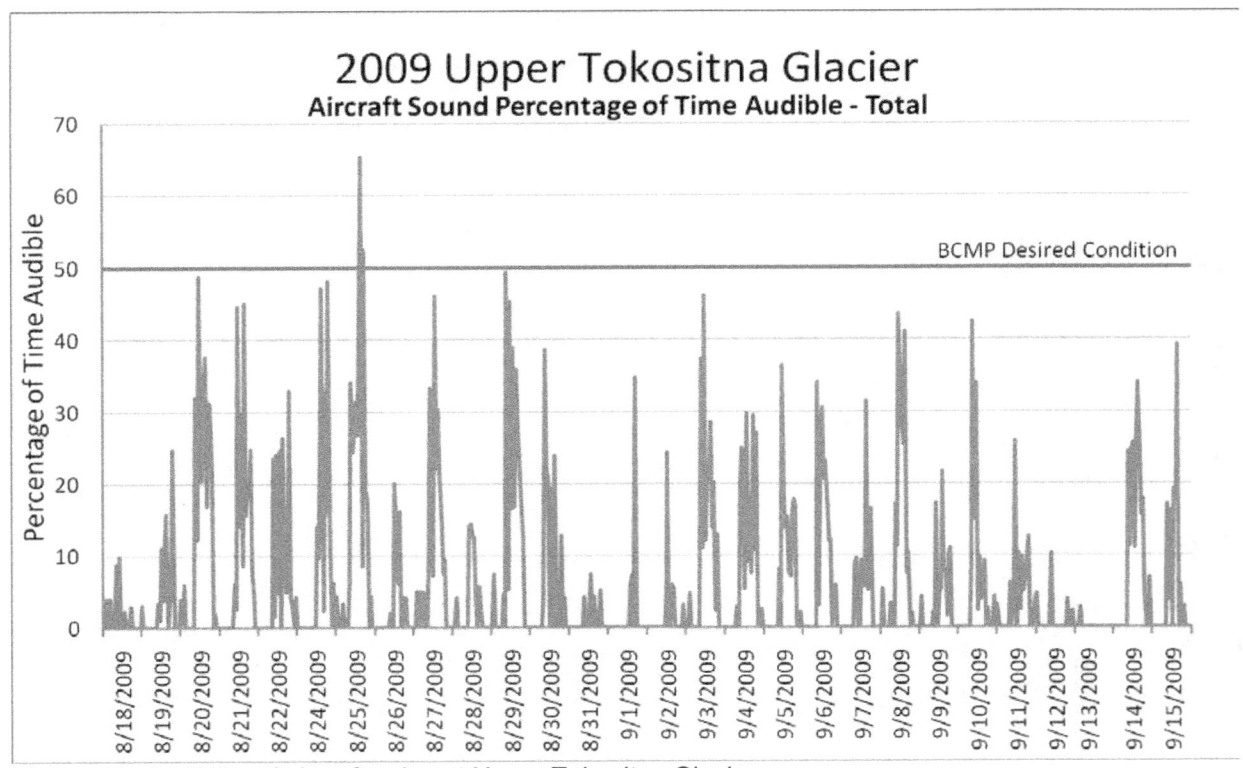

Figure 46. Audibility of aircraft noise at Upper Tokositna Glacier.

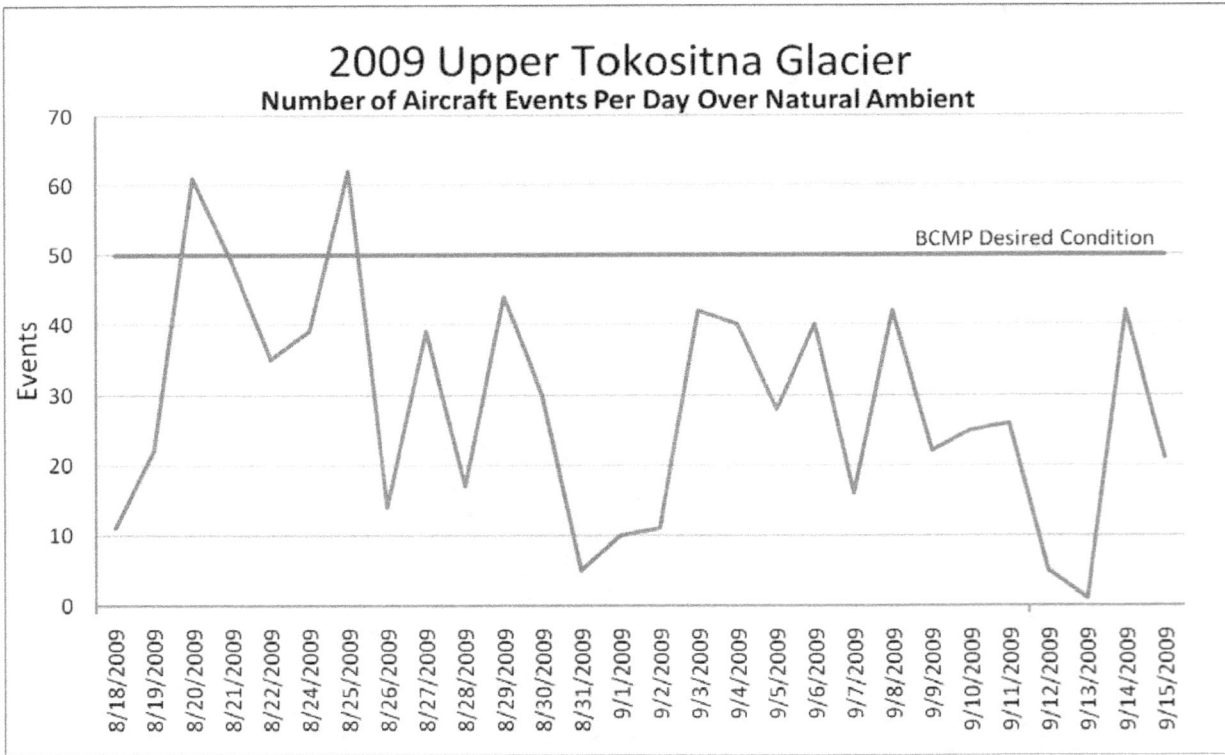

Figure 47. Number of aircraft noise events identified per day at Upper Tokositna Glacier.

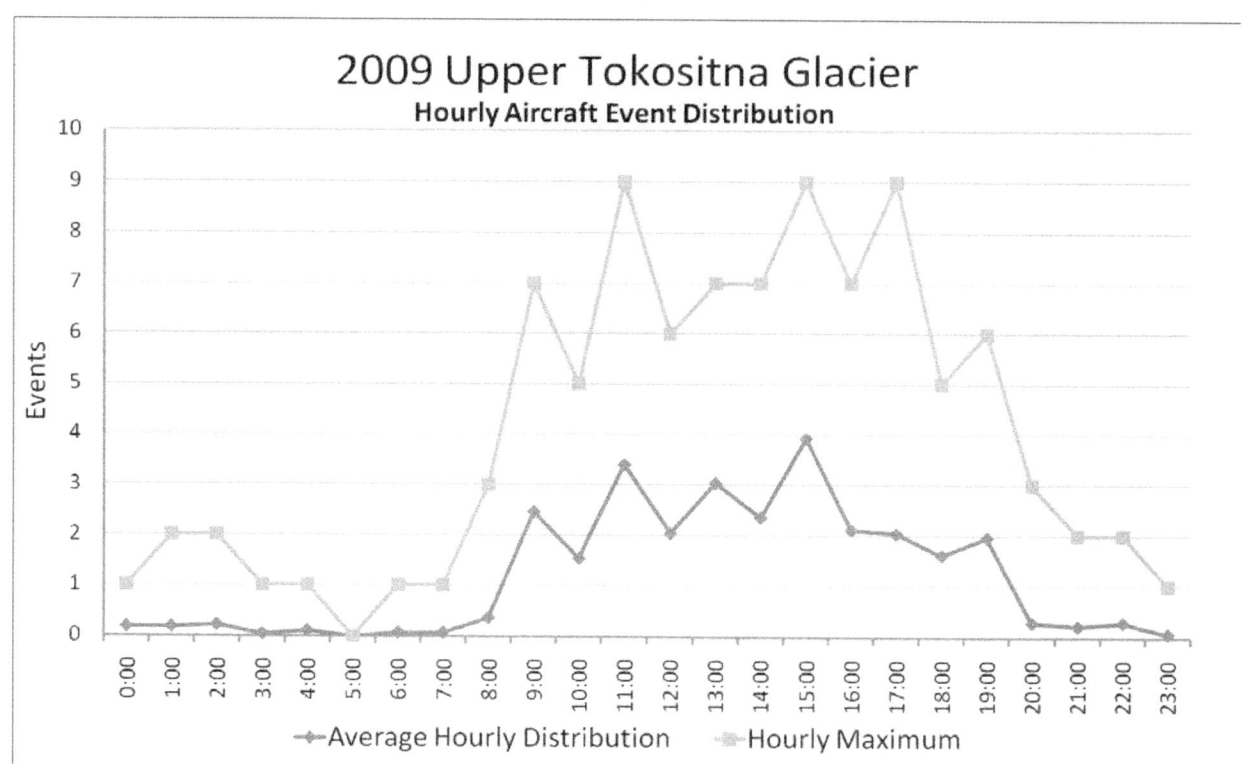

Figure 48. Hourly average and maximum aircraft event distribution at Upper Tokositna Glacier.

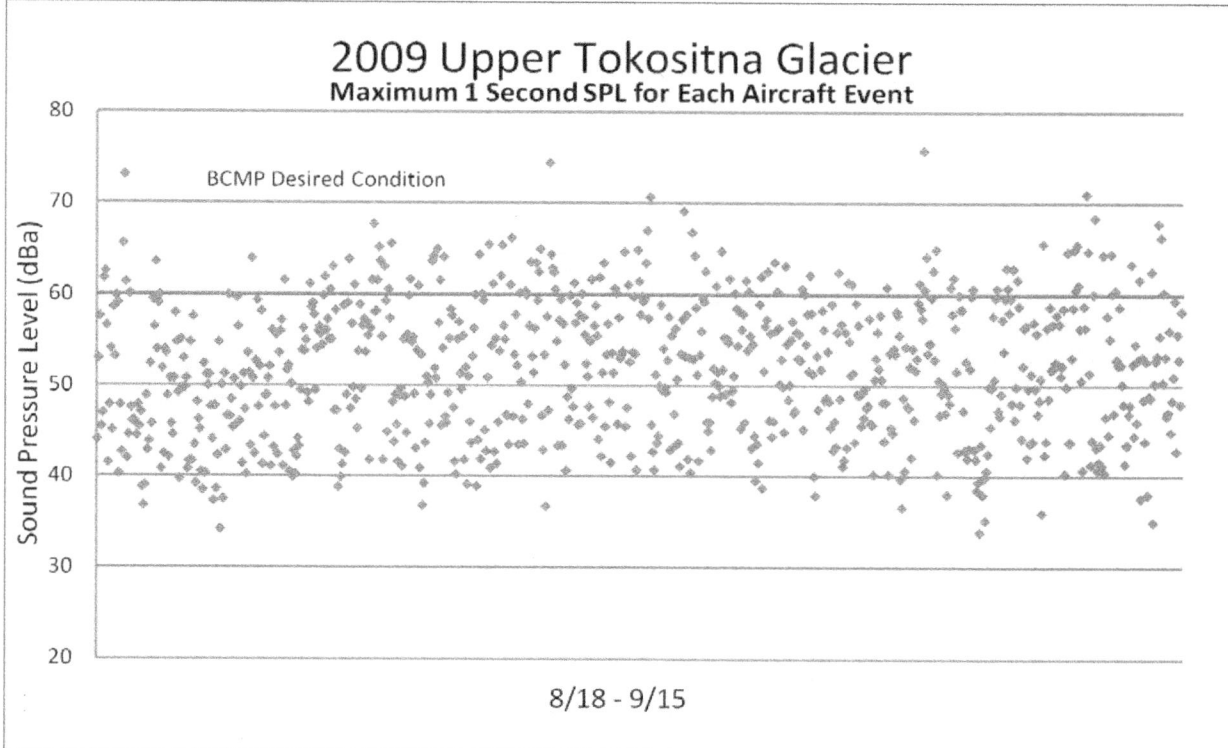

Figure 49. Maximum one-second SPL for each aircraft event identified at Upper Tokositna Glacier.

Upper Traleika Glacier

Location Description: At approximately 8000' elevation on the East Fork of the Upper Traleika Glacier.

Purpose/Project: Location randomly chosen from the LTEM grid as part of the long-term Denali Soundscape inventorying and monitoring sampling plan.

Coordinates: Lat. 63.07688, Long. 150.82539   Elevation: 2537 Meters

Time at Location: 10-June-2009 – 13-July-2009

BCMP Management Zone: Low   Park Ecoregion: Nonvegetated Alpine Mountains

Access: Helicopter

Summary: The purpose of the Upper Traleika Galcier location was to collect data at one of the long-term ecological monitoring (LTEM) grid points as outlined in the above sampling plan. LTEM grid point #80 was stratified as an Old Park location (designated Wilderness) and randomly selected from all locations requiring aircraft access.

This site was situated at high elevation and, due to cost and difficulty of access, was not allowed any maintenance visits. The equipment was packaged in a "lightweight" configuration using no solar panels and a pair of non-rechargeable dry cell alkaline "lantern" batteries. These batteries are factory rated at 52AH capacity, and were expected to power the site for approximately 25 days. Unfortunately, after the site was retrieved, it was found to have collected data for only 3 days before the batteries were depleted. The reason for this was that the battery manufacturer rates the batteries at a very, very low current draw, and the capacity degrades quickly as the current draw increases. Future installations should use six or more pairs of batteries wired in parallel to lower the current draw on each cell and thus achieve the rated capacity.

Results should be interpreted as a spot measurement of acoustic conditions that this site during a period of good weather. Not a comprehensive average profile as is possible with a longer duration data set.

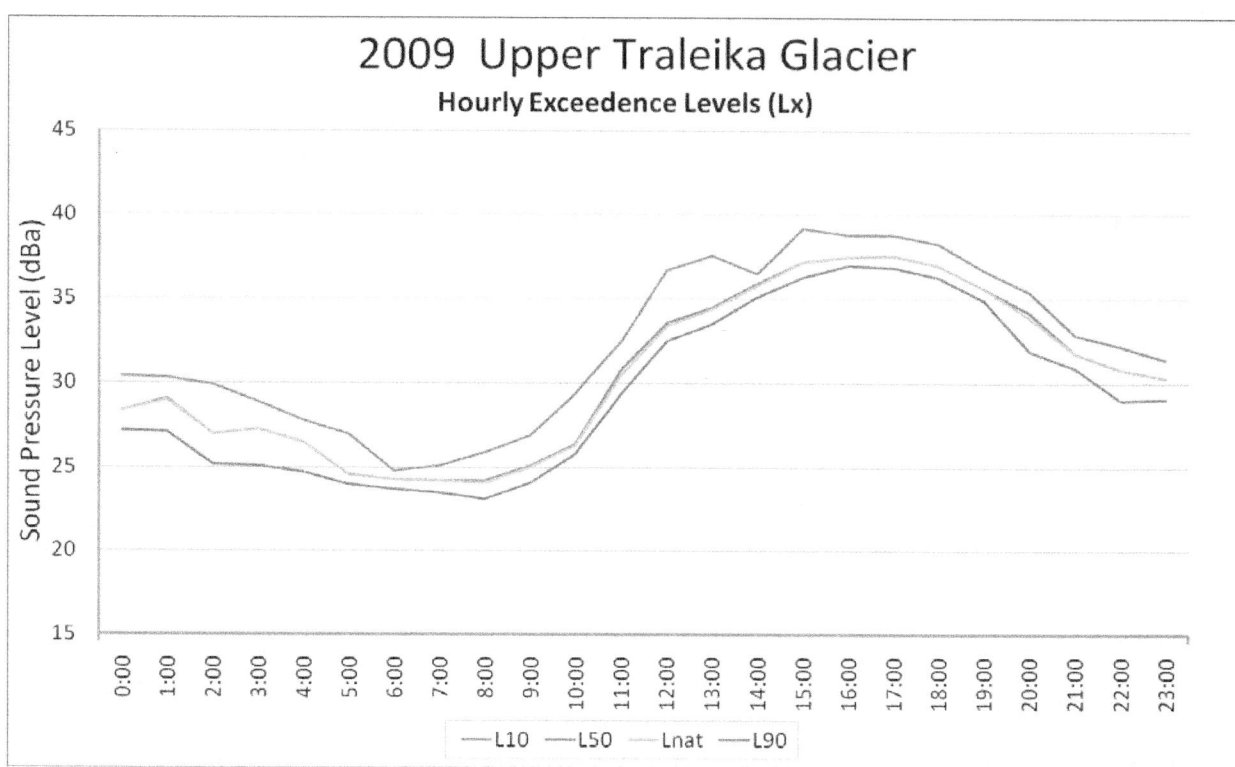

Figure 50. Exceedence levels for Upper Traleika Glacier.

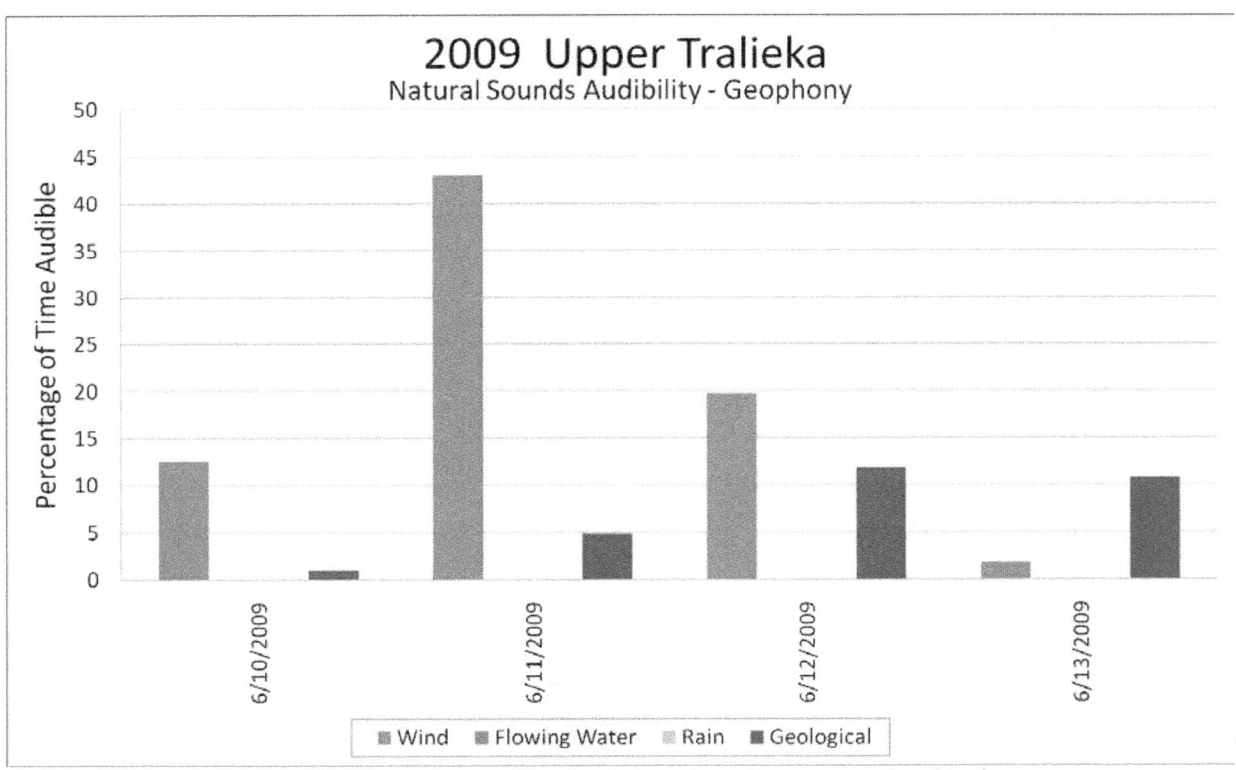

Figure 51. Percentage of time audible for geophonic sounds at Upper Traleika Glacier.

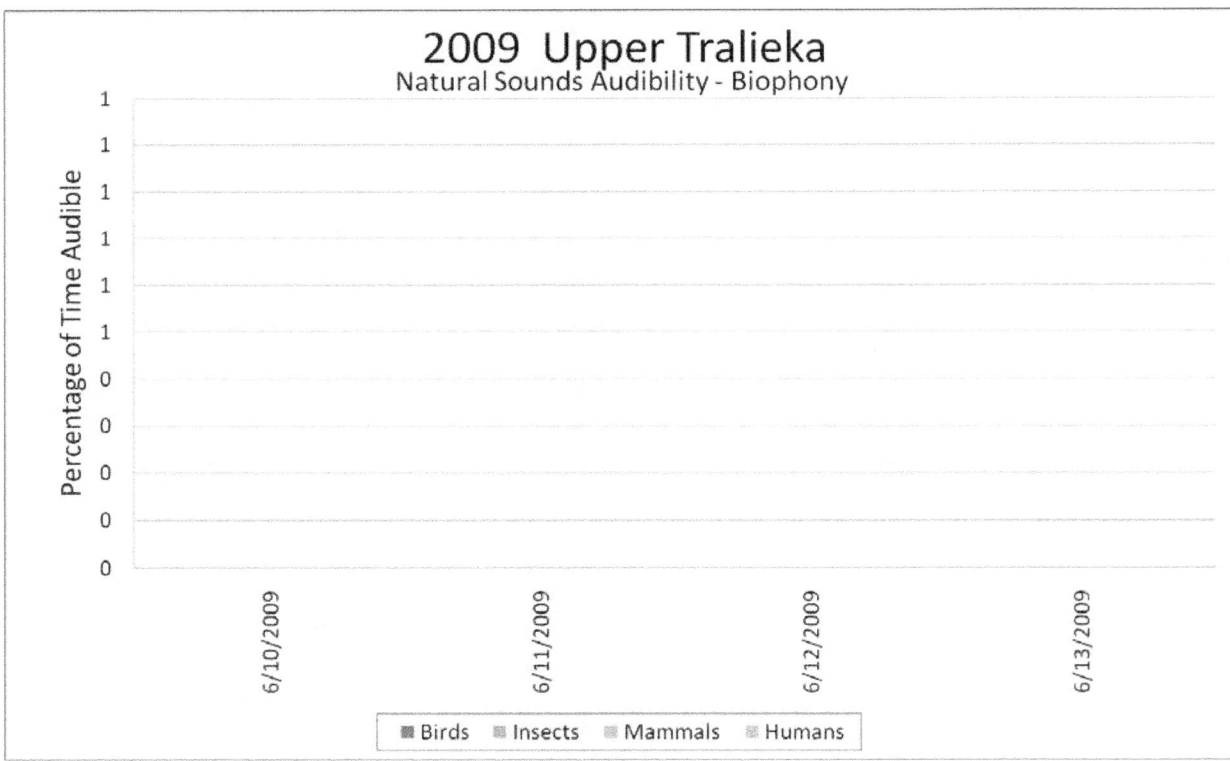

Figure 52. Percentage of time audible for biophonic sounds at Upper Traleika Glacier.

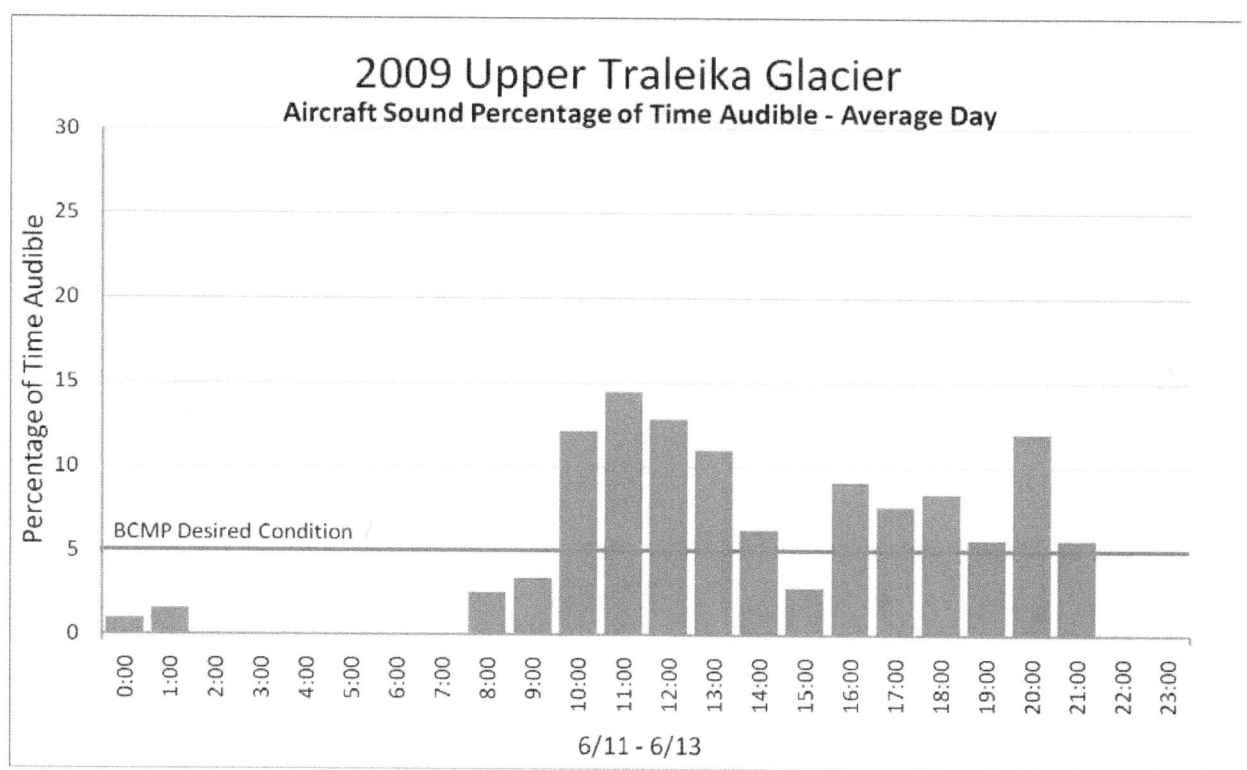

Figure 53. Audibility of aircraft noise for an average day, by hour, at Upper Traleika Glacier.

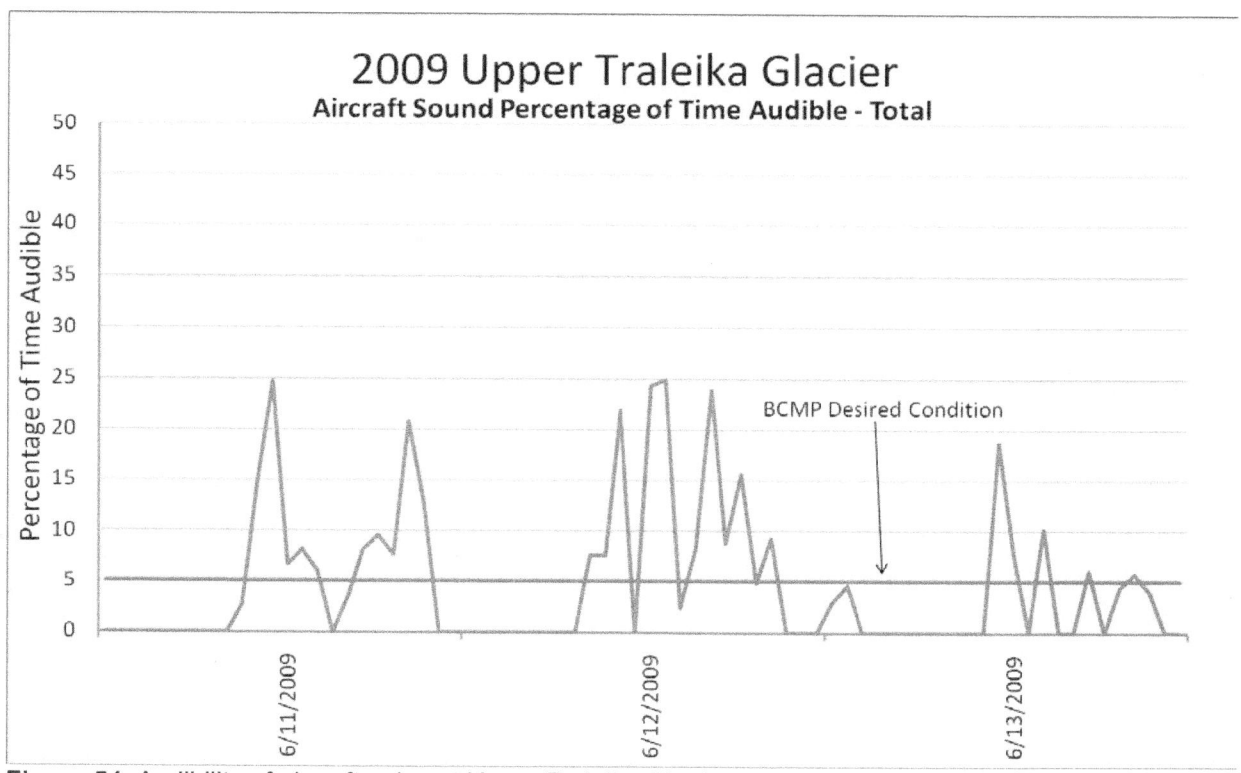

Figure 54. Audibility of aircraft noise at Upper Traleika Glacier.

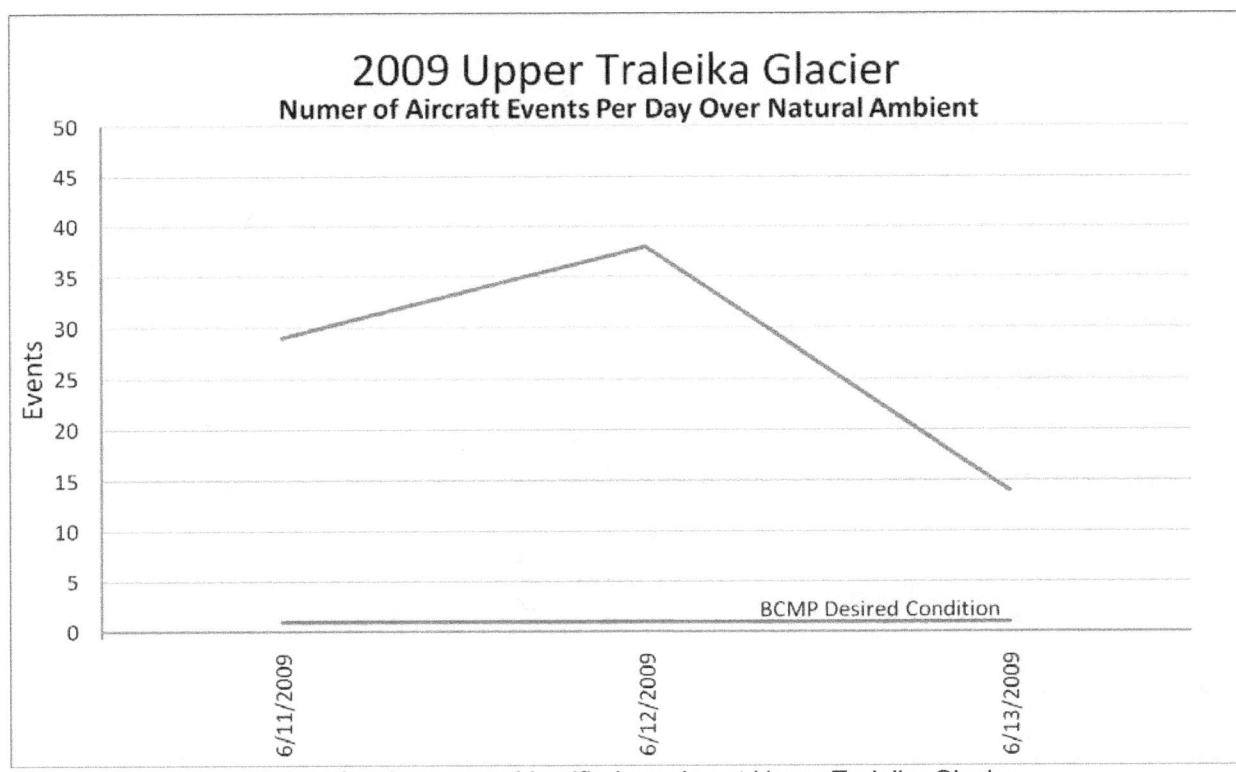

Figure 55. Number of aircraft noise events identified per day at Upper Traleika Glacier.

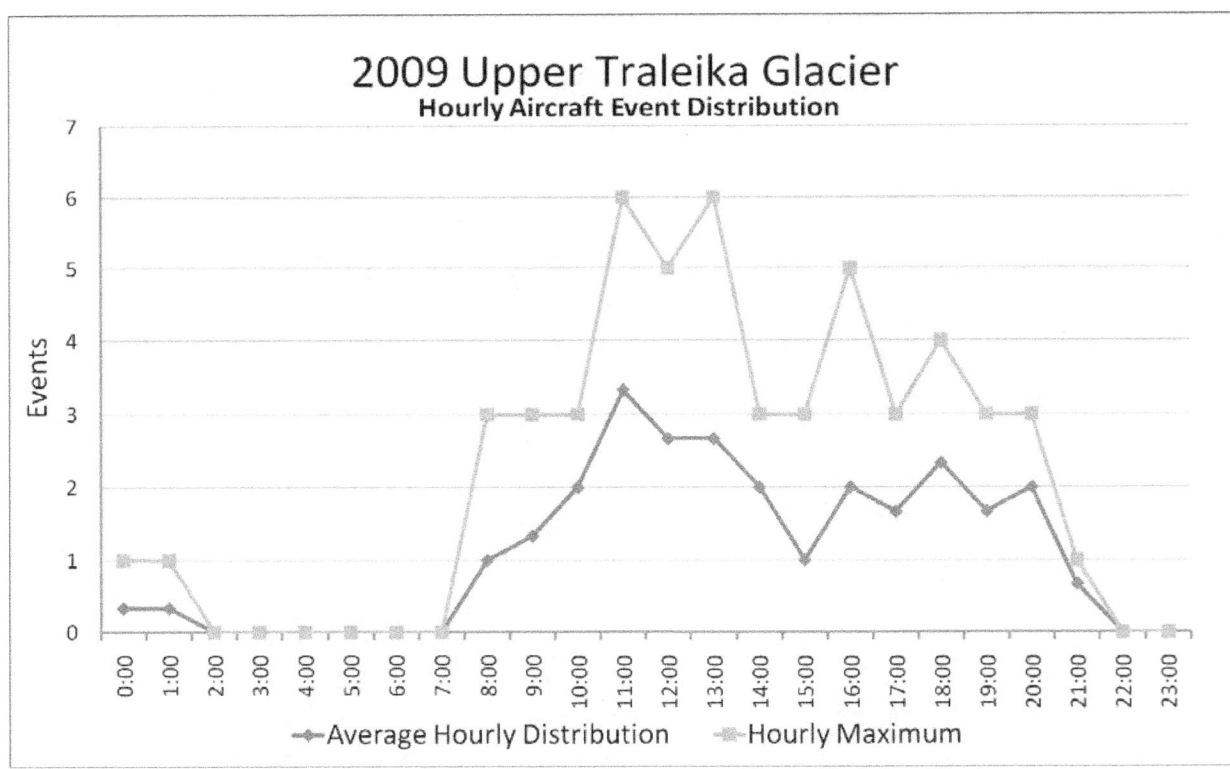

Figure 56. Hourly average and maximum for aircraft events at Upper Traleika Glacier.

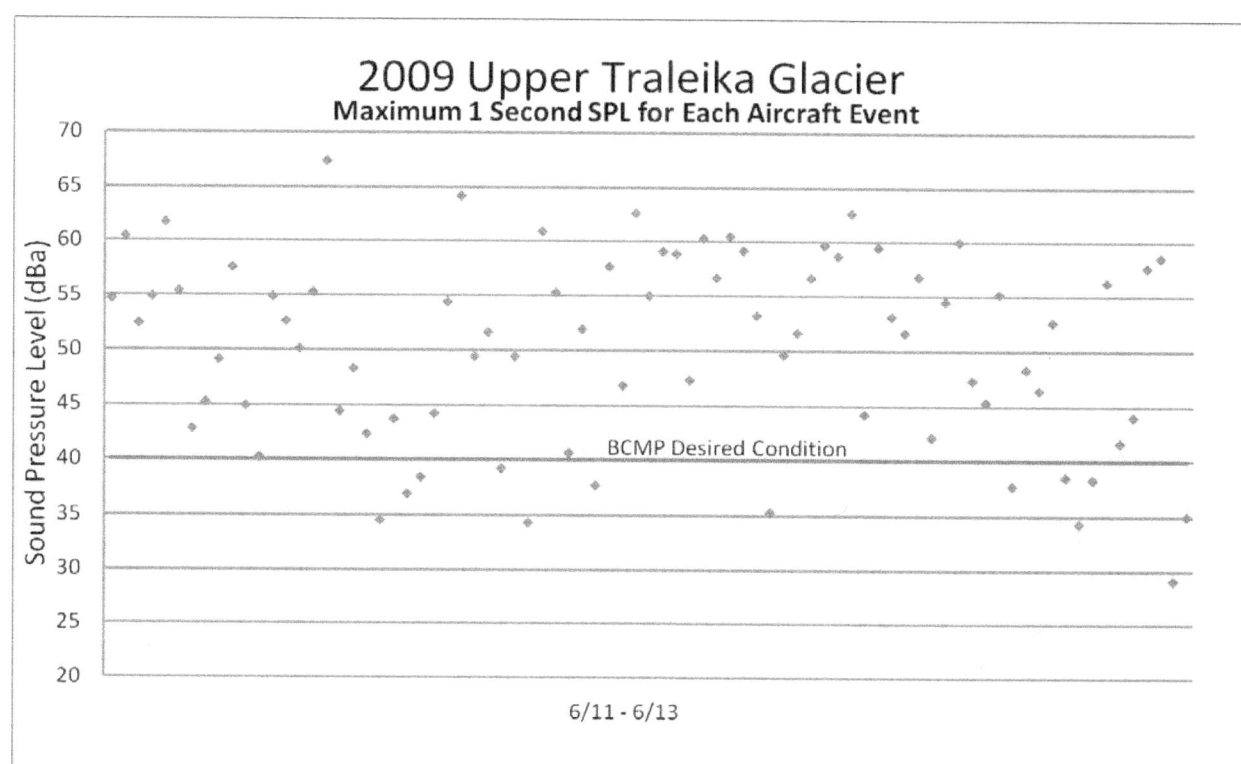

Figure 57. Maximum one-second SPL for each aircraft event identified at Upper Traleika Glacier.

Location Description: ~4km upstream along the east fork in the upper west branch of the Toklat River.

Purpose/Project: Location randomly chosen from the LTEM grid as part of the long-term Denali Soundscape inventorying and monitoring sampling plan.

Coordinates: Lat. 63.40927, Long. 150.03561   Elevation: 1224 Meters

Time at Location: 11-August-2009 – 7-Sept-2009

BCMP Management Zone: Low   Park Ecoregion: Alpine Mountains

Access: Foot

Summary: The purpose of the Upper West Branch Toklat location was to collect acoustic data at one of the long-term ecological monitoring (LTEM) grid points, as outlined in the above sampling plan. LTEM grid point #138 was stratified as an Old Park (designated Wilderness) location and randomly selected from all locations allowing access on foot.

The most commonly heard sounds at this site were wind (audible 43% of the time), rain (11%), arctic ground squirrels (9%), and birds (5%). Human made sound was audible 3.7% of the time on average.   Conditions exceeded the BCMP percent audible standard 28% of the time, number of events per day 100% of the time, and maximum SPL 89% of the time.

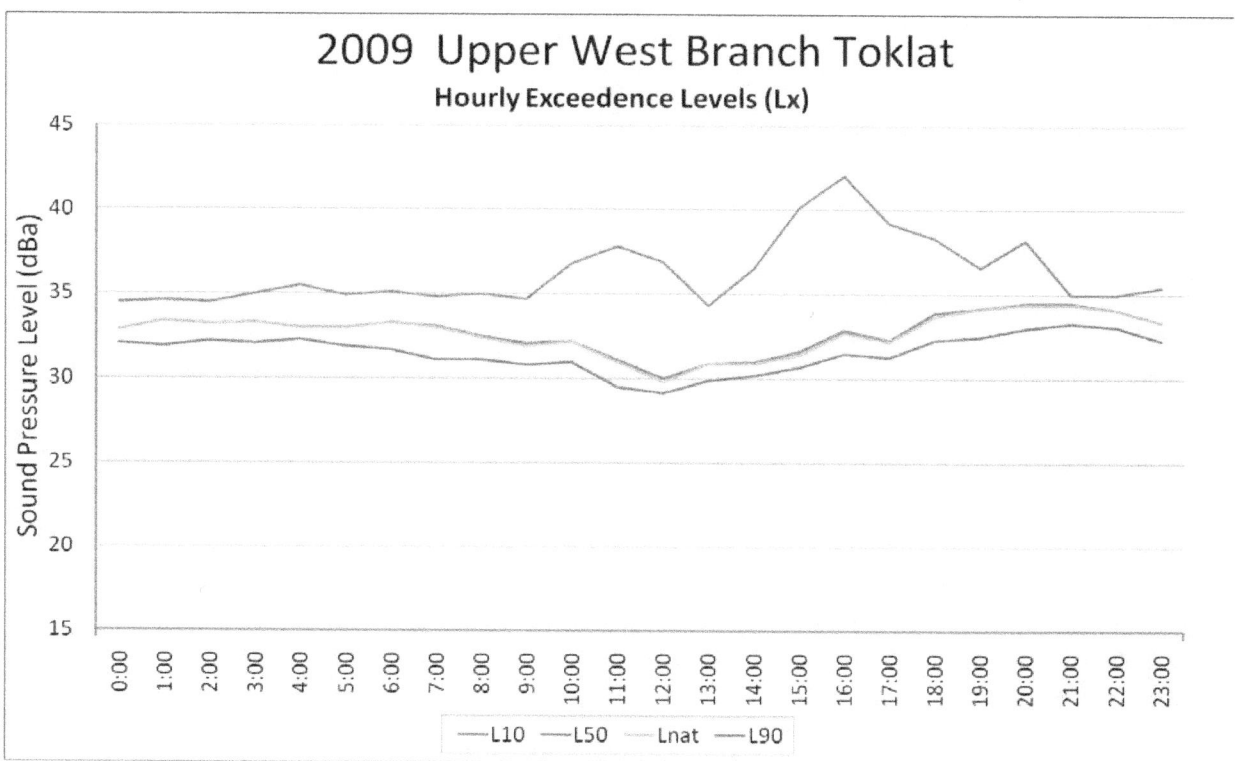

Figure 58. Exceedence levels for Upper West Branch Toklat.

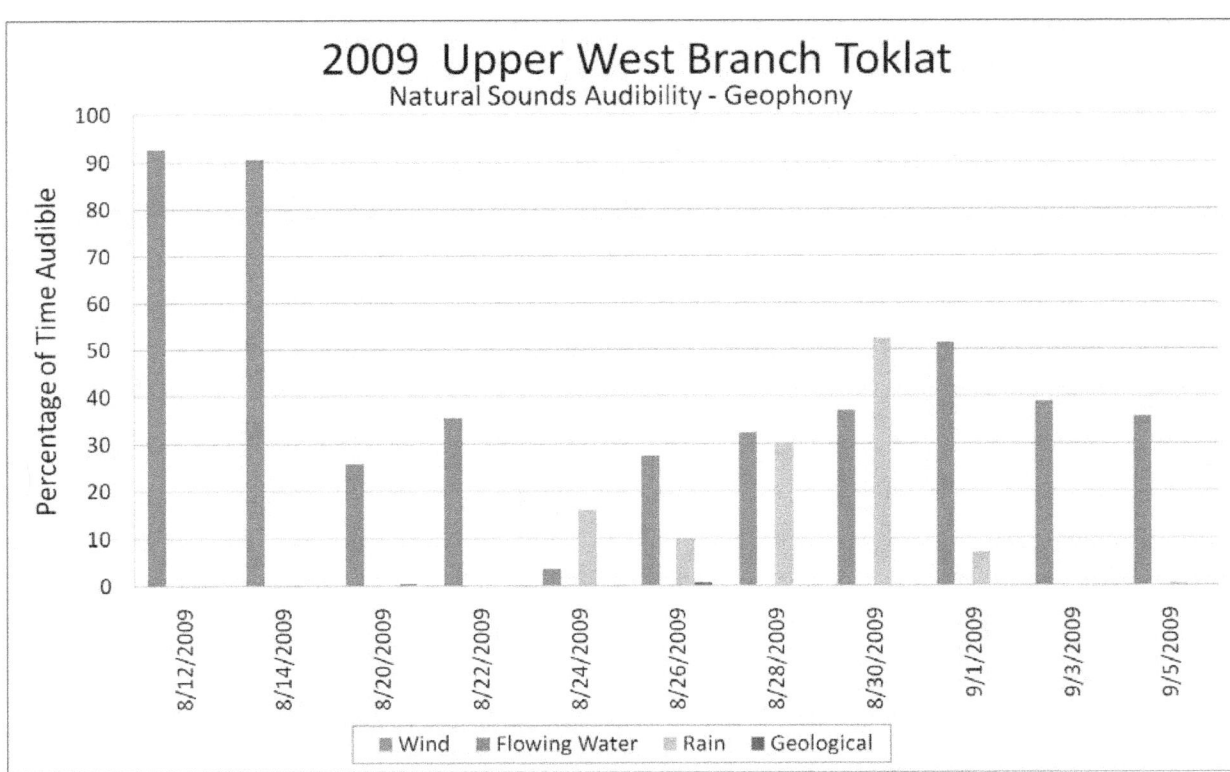

Figure 59. Percentage of time audible for geophonic sounds at Upper West Branch Toklat.

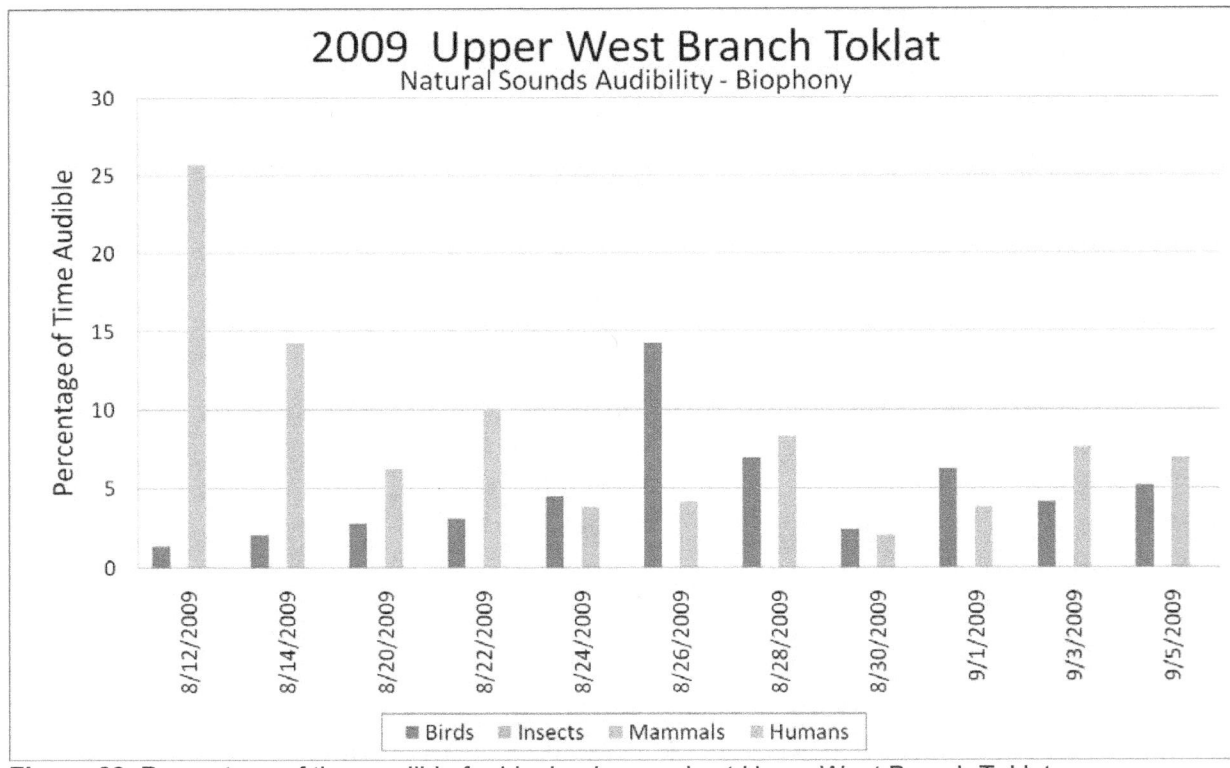

Figure 60. Percentage of time audible for biophonic sounds at Upper West Branch Toklat.

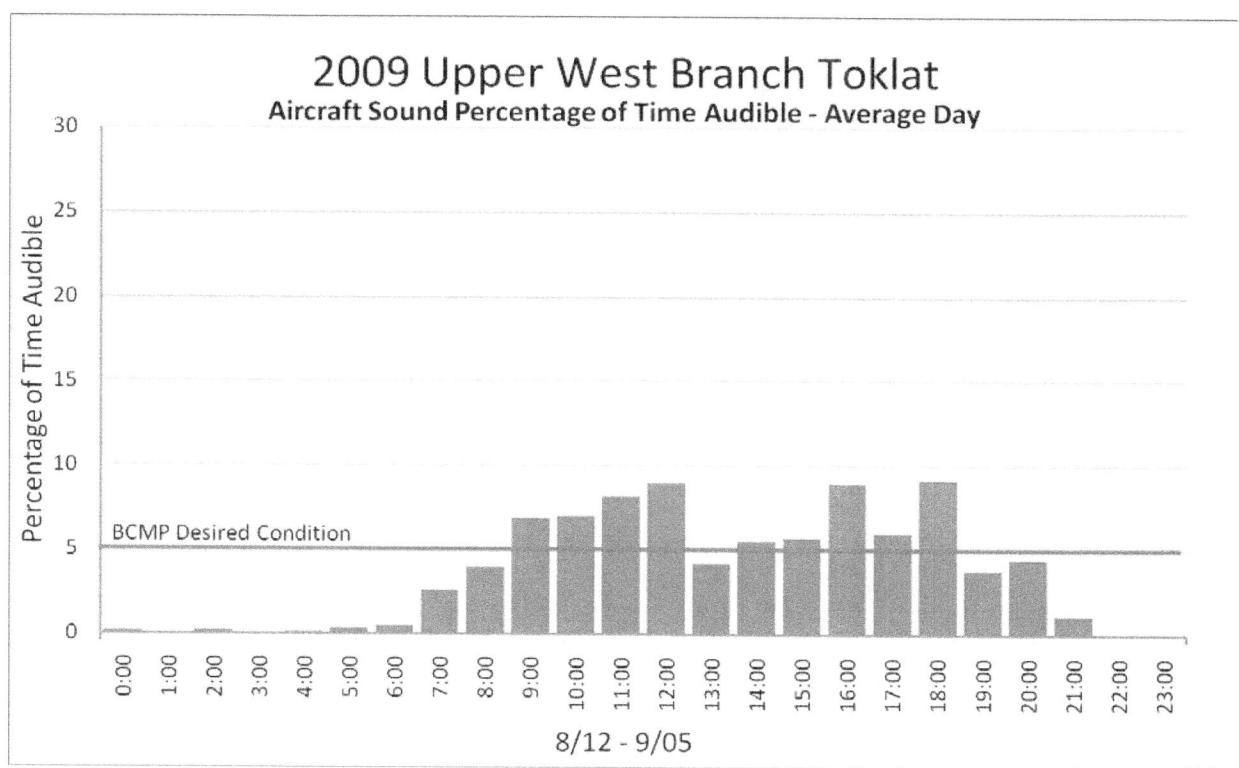

Figure 61. Audibility of aircraft noise for an average day, by hour, at Upper West Branch Toklat.

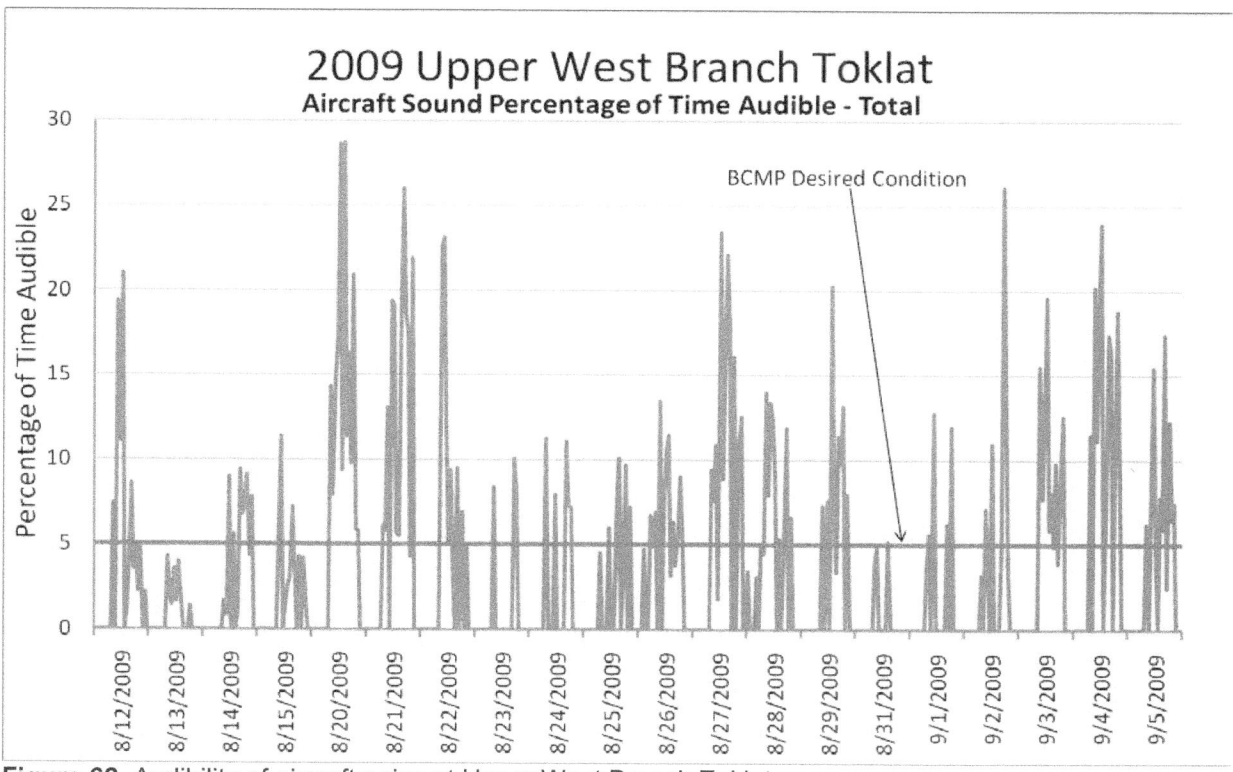

Figure 62. Audibility of aircraft noise at Upper West Branch Toklat.

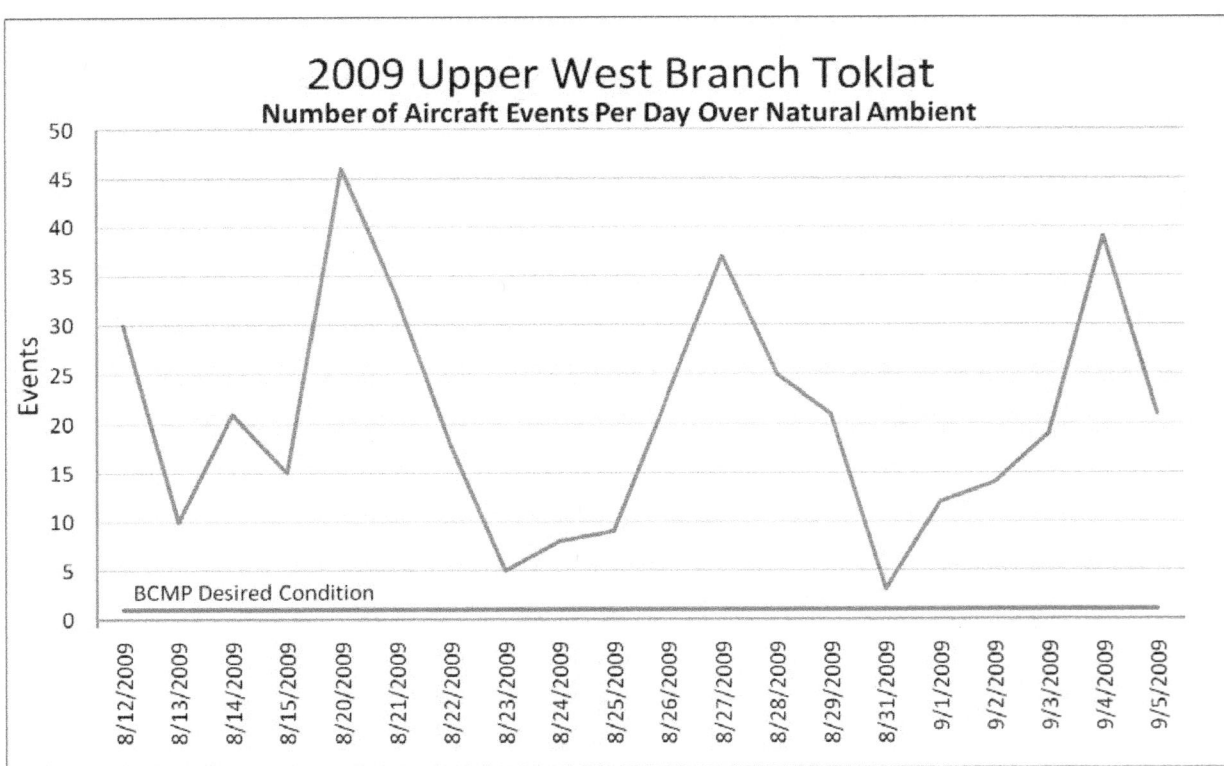

Figure 63. Number of aircraft noise events identified per day at Upper West Branch Toklat.

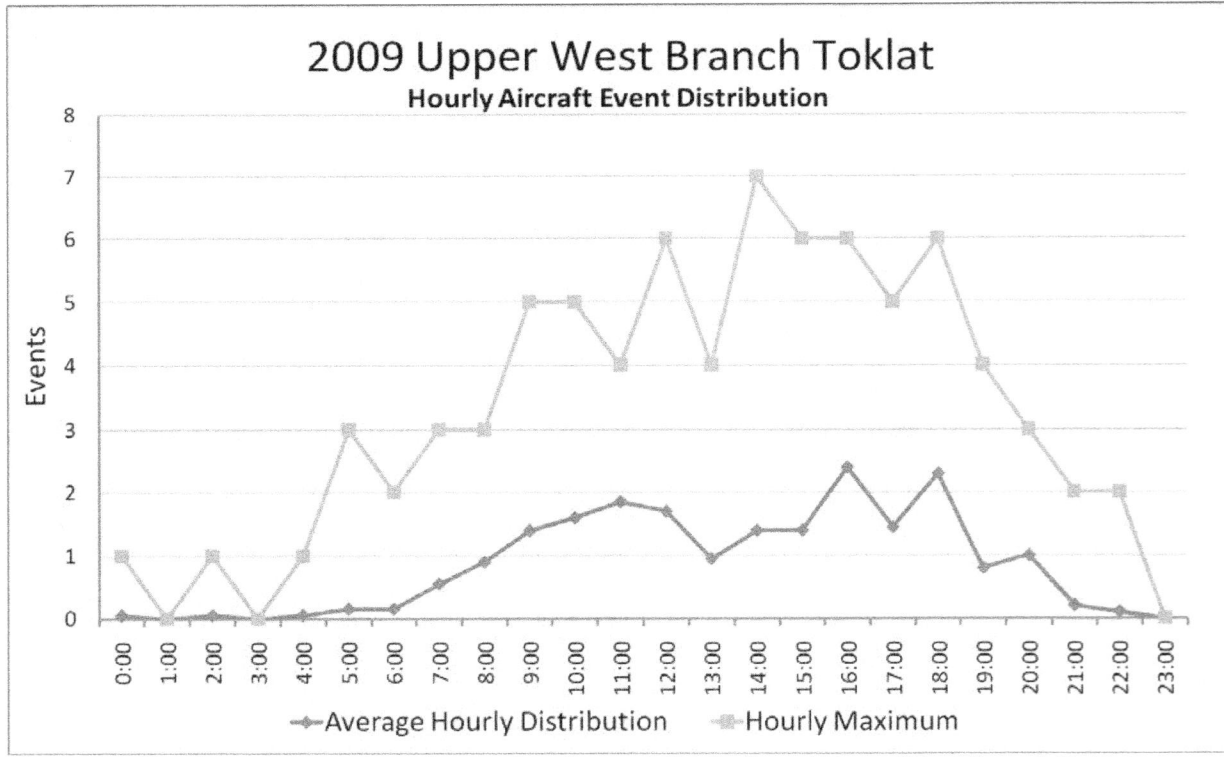

Figure 64. Hourly average and maximum aircraft event distribution at Upper West Branch Toklat.

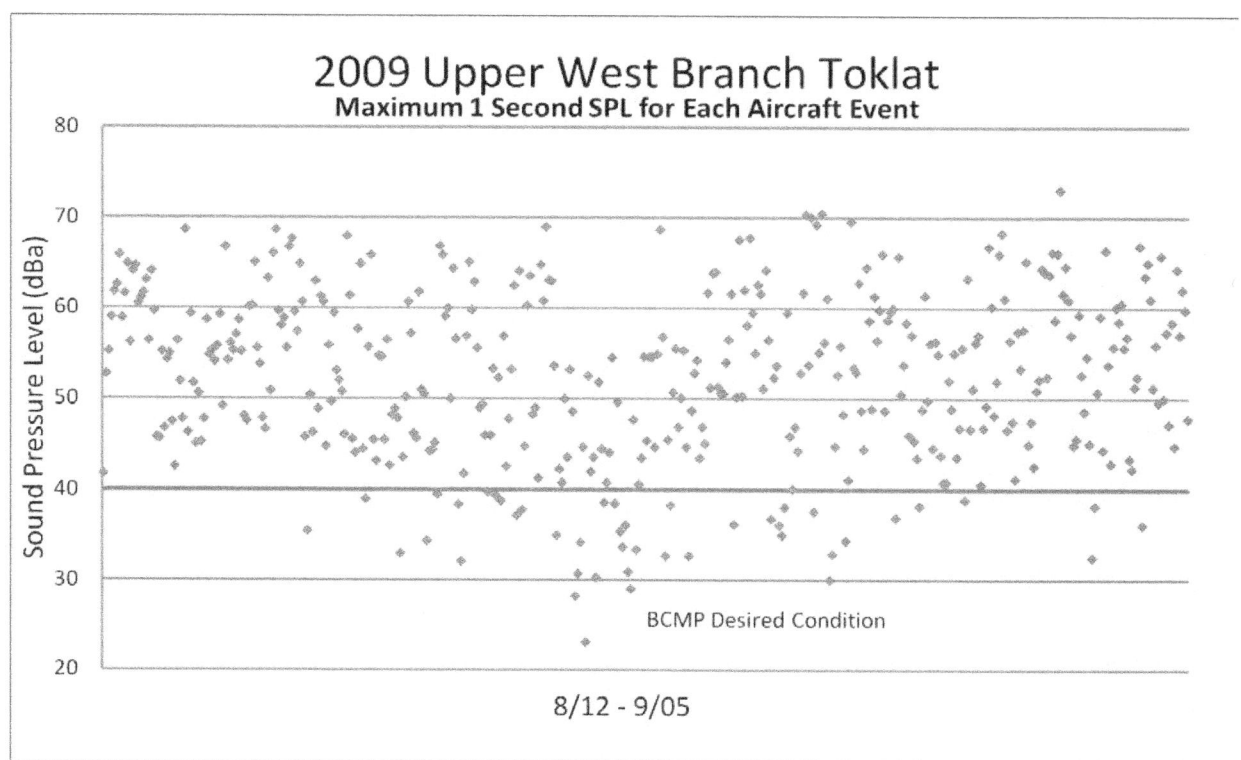

Figure 65. Maximum one-second SPL for each aircraft event identified at Upper West Branch Toklat.

Conclusion

The fourth year of the Denali Soundscape Inventory was intended to provide baseline natural sounds and current overflight data at an additional ten sites in Denali National Park and Preserve. It builds on previous work conducted 2001-2008, which collected similar data at other locations.

The acoustic monitoring systems collected detailed records of ambient sound pressure levels. The existing ambient (L_{50}) level is the median sound level, and is the composite of all sounds at a site, both human-caused and natural. Overall, the acoustic conditions of these 2009 sites varied. The Lower Slippery Creek site experienced the lowest ambient and natural ambient sound levels. Very low levels of aircraft activity were observed at Castle Rocks.   All sites exhibited some level of exceedence of the Denali Backcountry Management Plan standards as shown in Table 4. These findings have been added to the parkwide backcountry management plan compliance maps which can be found in Appendix B.

Table 4. Percentage of samples exceeding BCMP sound standards.

Site Name	Hourly Motorized Noise Audiblity	Motorized Noise Events/Day	Motorized Max SPL (dBA)
North Vertical Angle BM	7	61	35
Center Alaska	23	100	55
Dunkle Hills[1]	*	*	*
Herron River	8	57	31
Lower Slippery Creek	18	94	19
Triple Lakes	65	100	64
Upper Tokositna Glacier	0	7	15
Upper Traleika Glacier	35	100	84
Upper West Branch Toklat	28	100	89

[1] : Winter season site.
*: Collection of SPL data was unsuccessful. This precludes calculation of BCMP indicator metrics.

As it stands today, Denali National Park and Preserve has one of the most extensive acoustical monitoring datasets in the National Park system. The data included in this report may be used to inform a Soundscape Management Plan, General Management Plan, Resource Stewardship Strategy, Natural Resource Conditions Assessment, other park plans, or NEPA documents that include soundscapes.

Literature Cited

American National Standards Institute (ANSI). 1992. Quantities and procedures for description and measurement of environmental sound. Part 2: Measurement of long-term, wide-area sound. Accredited Standards Committee S12, Noise. Acoustical Society of America, New York, NY.

American National Standards Institute (ANSI). 1968. Audiometer Standard 3.6.

Ambrose, S., and S. Burson, S. 2004. Soundscape Studies in National Parks. George Wright Forum 21(1): 29-38

Dunholter, P.A., V. Mestre, R. Harris, and L. Cohn. 1989. Methodology for the measurement of and analysis of aircraft sound levels within national parks. Unpublished report to National Park Service, Contract No. CX 8000-7-0028. Mestre Greve Associates, Newport Beach, CA.

Hults, C. 2005. Denali National Park and Preserve Soundscape Annual Report 2005. National Park Service Internal Document.

Lee, Cynthia, et. al. 2006. Baseline Ambient Sound Levels in Haleakalā National Park. Cambridge, MA: John A. Volpe National Transportation Systems Center Acoustics Facility.

National Park Service. 1916. Organic Act (16 U.S.C 1 2 3 and 4).

National Park Service. 1978. Redwood Act (92 STAT. 163).

National Park Service. 2000. Director's Order #47. Soundscape Preservation and Noise Management.

National Park Service. 2006a. Management Policy 4.9: Soundscape Management.

National Park Service. 2006b. Management Policy 8.2.3: Use of Motorized Equipment.

National Park Service. 2006c. Denali National Park and Preserve Final Backcountry Management Plan, Environmental Impact Statement. National Park Service.

National Park Service. 2008. Haleakalā National Park Acoustic Monitoring Report. Natural Resource Report NPS/NRPC NRTR—2008/001. National Park Service, Fort Collins, CO.

Withers, J. and C. Hults. 2006. Denali National Park and Preserve Soundscape Annual Report 2006. National Park Service Internal Document.

Withers, J. 2009. Denali National Park and Preserve Soundscape Annual Report 2008. National Park Service Internal Document.

Withers, J. 2008. Denali National Park and Preserve Soundscape Annual Report 2007. National Park Service Internal Document.

Appendix A. Glossary of Acoustic Terms

Acoustical Environment

The actual physical sound resources, regardless of audibility, at a particular location.

Amplitude

The instantaneous magnitude of an oscillating quantity such as sound pressure. The peak amplitude is the maximum value.

Audibility

The ability of animals with normal hearing, including humans, to hear a given sound. Audibility is affected by the hearing ability of the animal, the masking effects of other sound sources, and by the frequency content and amplitude of the sound.

dBA

A-weighted decibel. A-weighted sum of sound energy across the range of human hearing. Humans do not hear well at very low or very high frequencies. Weighting adjusts for this.

Decibel (dB)

A logarithmic measure of acoustic or electrical signals. The formula for computing decibels is: 10(Log10(sound level/reference sound level)). 0 dB represents the lowest sound level that can be perceived by a human with healthy hearing. Conversational speech is about 65 dB.

Extrinsic Sound

Any sound not forming an essential part of the park unit, or a sound originating from outside the park boundary.

Frequency

The number of times per second that the sine wave of sound repeats itself. It can be expressed in cycles per second, or Hertz (Hz). Frequency equals Speed of Sound/ Wavelength.

Hearing Range (frequency)

By convention, an average, healthy, young person is said to hear frequencies from approximately 20Hz to 20000 Hz.

Hertz (Hz)

A measure of frequency, or the number of pressure variations per second. A person with normal hearing can hear between 20 Hz and 20,000 Hz.

Human-Caused Sound

Any sound that is attributable to a human source.

Intrinsic sound

A sound which belongs to a park by its very nature, based on the park unit purposes, values, and establishing legislation. The term "intrinsic sounds" has replaced "natural sounds" in order to incorporate both cultural and historic sounds as part of the acoustic environment of a park.

Listening Horizon

The range or limit of one's hearing capabilities. Just as smog limits the visual horizon, so noise limits the acoustic horizon.

L_{eq}

Energy Equivalent Sound Level. The level of a constant sound over a specific time period that has the same sound energy as the actual (unsteady) sound over the same period.

L_x

A metric used to describe acoustic data. It represents the level of sound exceeded x percent of the time during the given measurement period. Thus, L_{50} is the level exceeded 50% of the time (it is also referred to as existing ambient).

L_{nat}

An estimate of what the acoustical environment might sound like without the contribution of extrinsic (anthropogenic) sounds.

Masking

The process by which the threshold of audibility for a sound is raised by the presence of another sound.

Noise-Free Interval

The period of time between noise events (not silence).

Noise

Sound which is unwanted, either because of its effects on humans, its effect on fatigue or malfunction of physical equipment, or its interference with the perception or detection of other sounds (Source: McGraw Hill Dictionary of Scientific and Technical Terms).

Off-site Listening

The systematic identification of sound sources using digital recordings previously collected in the field.

Sound

Variations in local pressure that propagate through a medium (e.g. the atmosphere) in space and time.

Soundscape

Human perception of the acoustical environment.

Sound Pressure

The difference between instantaneous pressure and local barometric pressure. Measured in Pascals (Pa), Newtons per square meter, which is the metric equivalent of pounds per square inch.

Sound Pressure Level (SPL)

A calibrated measure of sound level, expressed in decibels, and referred to an atmospheric standard of 20 micro Pascals.

Time Audible

The amount of time that a sound source is audible to a human with normal hearing.

Appendix B. BCMP Exceedence Maps

The following three maps are compiled to provide a parkwide look at the acoustic measurements made to date, and indicate the current level compliance with BCMP acoustic standards. There is one map for each BCMP standard, and each sampling point is annotated with the percentage of time that standard was exceeded during the measurement period. Data from previous years is from Hults 2005, Withers and Hults 2006, and Withers 2009.

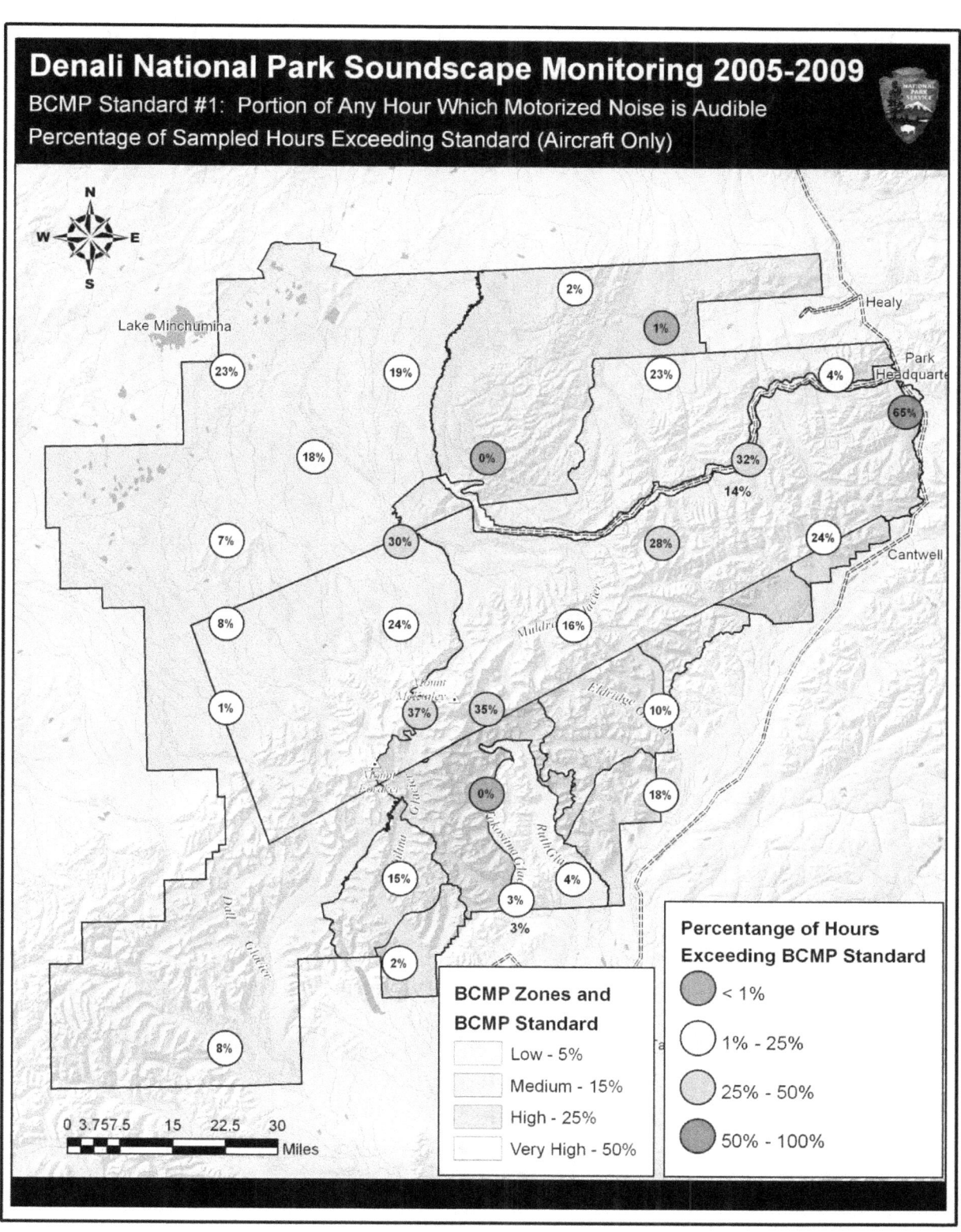

Denali National Park Soundscape Monitoring 2005-2009

BCMP Standard #1: Portion of Any Hour Which Motorized Noise is Audible
Percentage of Sampled Hours Exceeding Standard (Aircraft Only)

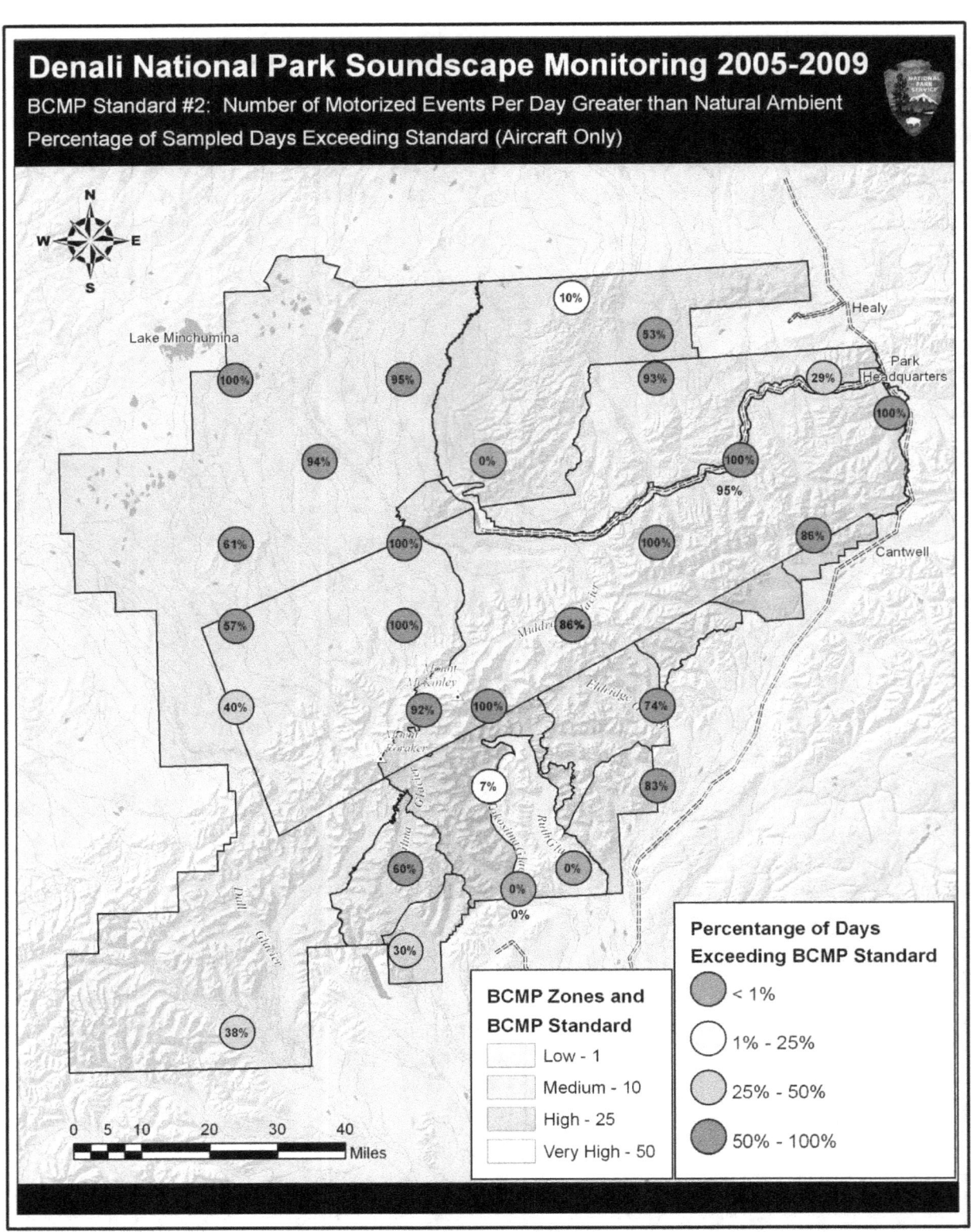

Denali National Park Soundscape Monitoring 2005-2009

BCMP Standard #2: Number of Motorized Events Per Day Greater than Natural Ambient

Percentage of Sampled Days Exceeding Standard (Aircraft Only)

Healy

Lake Minchumina

Park Headquarters

Cantwell

Mount McKinley

Mount Foraker

Muldrow Glacier

Eldridge Glacier

Ruth Glacier

Tokositna Glacier

Kahiltna Glacier

Pall Glacier

BCMP Zones and BCMP Standard

	Low - 1
	Medium - 10
	High - 25
	Very High - 50

Percentange of Days Exceeding BCMP Standard

- < 1%
- 1% - 25%
- 25% - 50%
- 50% - 100%

10% 53% 93% 29% 100% 100% 95% 86% 100% 95% 100% 100% 94% 61% 57% 40% 100% 100% 92% 100% 86% 74% 83% 7% 0% 0% 0% 60% 30% 38%

0   5   10   20   30   40
Miles

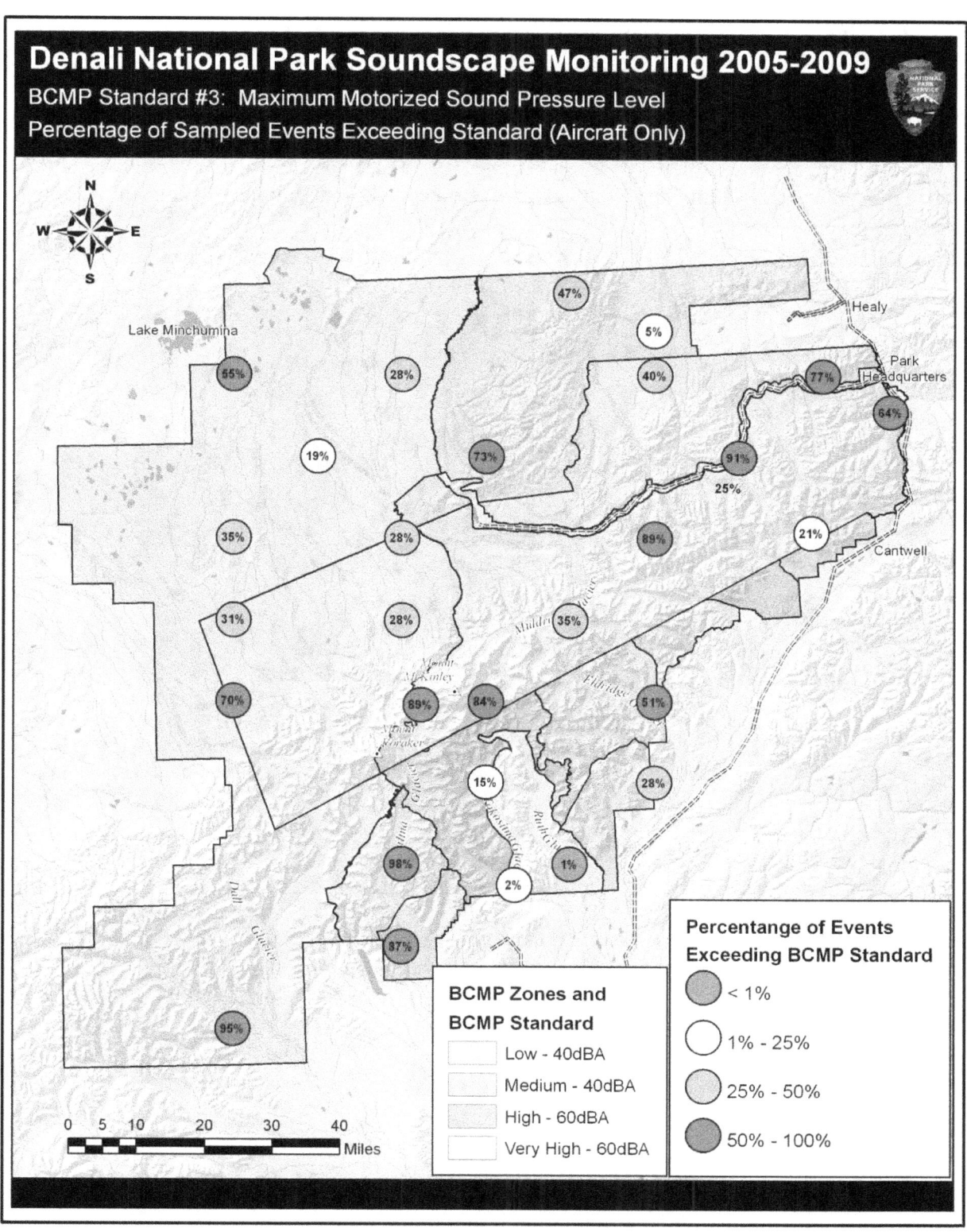

Denali National Park Soundscape Monitoring 2005-2009
BCMP Standard #3: Maximum Motorized Sound Pressure Level
Percentage of Sampled Events Exceeding Standard (Aircraft Only)

BCMP Zones and
BCMP Standard

- Low - 40dBA
- Medium - 40dBA
- High - 60dBA
- Very High - 60dBA

Percentange of Events
Exceeding BCMP Standard

- < 1%
- 1% - 25%
- 25% - 50%
- 50% - 100%

Appendix C. Analyzing audio with visual tools

Sound pressure levels (SPL) from one hour at an acoustic monitoring site at Haleakala National Park are shown below (Lee, 2006). One hour of SPL data is displayed over four rows. Each row shows SPL values from low frequency (12.5 Hz, bottom of line) to high frequency (20 kHz, top of line). Values are represented with a color scale, where dark blue is quiet and yellow/white is loud. Thus, individual events stand out against the blue background, appearing as yellow areas.

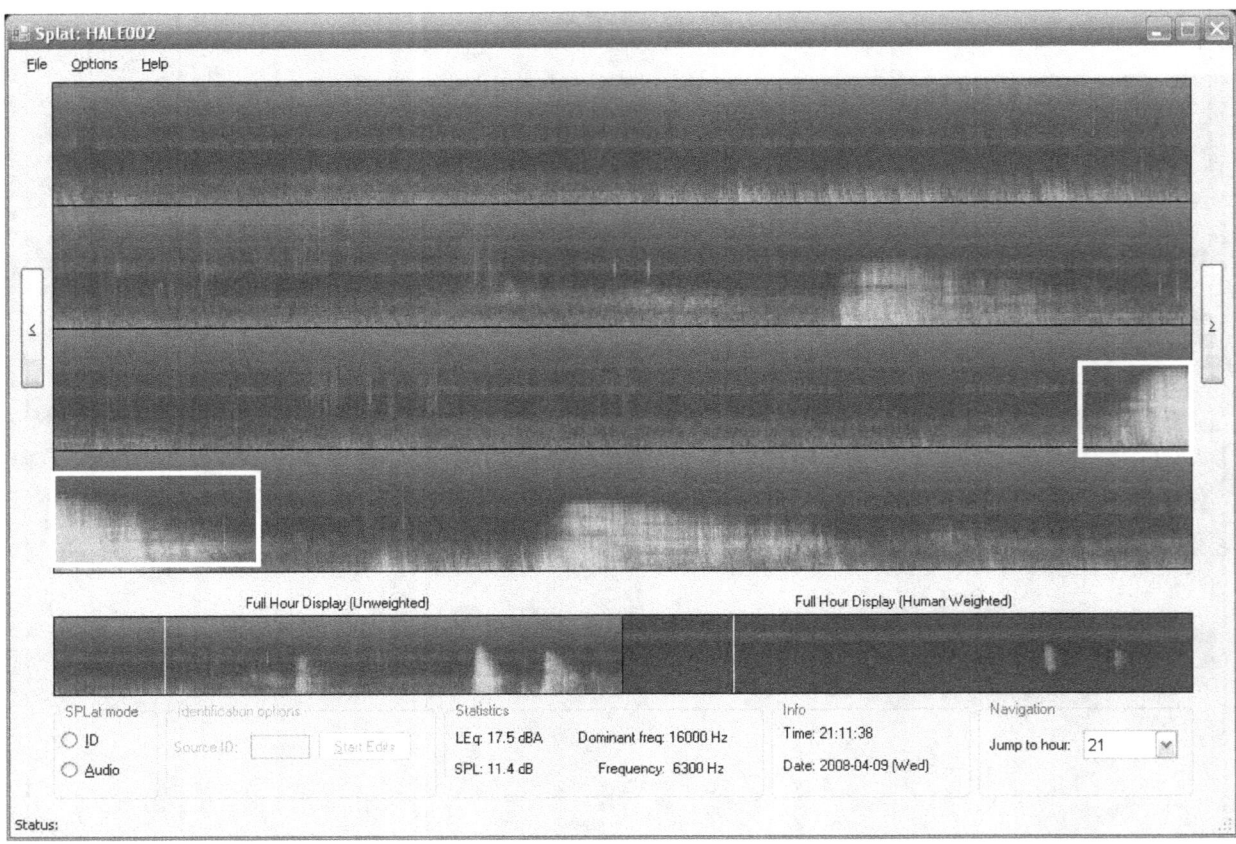

Acoustic events can be visually identified (by drawing a box around the event) and annotated. For each identified event, time, duration, maximum SPL, and spectral information are cataloged. For example, the white boxes above mark the occurrence of a high altitude jet overflight. Two other jet events are also visible.